MEN
WITH ADULT
ADHD

The Efficient Playbook to Break Free From Feelings of Failure, Improve Focus, Understand Executive Dysfunction, and Master Key Habits and Exercises For Executive Function Skills

CALVIN CAUFIELD

Table of Contents

Introduction

I'm running in the middle of a marathon. Pounding the pavement one step after another. I feel exhausted. My chest is heaving as I think, "how many more miles do I have left in me?"

Even catching up and sticking to the tempo of the runners around me feels way harder than it should be. Winning and getting ahead feels impossible. But I'm not just running a marathon. I'm running it with an overwhelmingly heavy backpack, filled with a dense weight dragging me back with every step I make.

This is what it feels like to live with ADHD.

Everyone has felt the weight of ADHD, but not all men are in the same part of their journey. If you are in the first group, you are just starting your productivity journey and personal growth, and all the content online is likely leaving you very overwhelmed.

If you are in the second group, you have already binged a massive amount of productivity content on social media and read countless books on goal setting, time management, willpower, motivation, purpose, career development, and hustling. After that, you began to experiment while imagining yourself as a disciplined navy seal, a hungry entrepreneur, or a productivity-maximizing rockstar.

Waking up early. Having cold showers. Working out. Running. Reflecting on your priorities and goals. Finding your life-changing WHY. Disappearing from social circles and going monk mode. Doing gratitude journaling. Trying to hustle with side gigs and freelancing. Think of any masculine, healthy, and productive habit, routine, and system, and you've likely tried many of them at some point.

No matter which group you're in, making progress feels impossible. Routines collapse. Habits disappear and get forgotten. Systems feel too restrictive and suffocating, and you abandon them. You've tried every possible strategy only to return to zero.

If you have recently been diagnosed with ADHD or suspect you may have the condition, you've come to the right place. To some degree, you likely struggle with the following:

- A history of losses, regrets, and missed opportunities due to impulsivity and spontaneous thinking
- Low self-worth and a haunting sense you are not being enough or tapping into your full potential
- Inability to regulate your attention, leaving you either distracted and zoning out or hyper-fixated with no way of snapping out
- Prioritizing, managing your time effectively, and staying committed to your goals long-term even when motivation runs low

- Keeping your emotions and mood in check due to a fiery temper, mood swings, and chronic frustration
- Opening up to your partner and maturely handling constructive criticism, disagreements, and rejections in relationships

Those are the problems, and I'm sure you've been trying your best to solve them or at least make some improvements. However, there is only so much progress you can make without acknowledging your ADHD and designing your life in a way compatible with your condition.

To avoid addressing your neurodivergence is like someone offering you advice on your running posture while you are out of breath due to the weight on your shoulders. Sure, maybe you could improve your running form, but the much bigger and more pressing problem is the ridiculously unbearable weight sinking you to the ground and making your feet drag instead of fly.

The premise of this book couldn't be simpler. We will do an in-depth dive into every aspect of your ADHD - the core symptoms, overlooked problems of males with ADHD, how the conditions affect your personal, professional, social, and dating life, and how to customize your habits, routines, and systems to be compatible with your unique brain.

The premise is simple, but what you will learn is far from the surface-level advice you'd receive if you were to quickly skim through Google results. I will not promise an overnight change, or a grandiose transformation. But, by the end of this book you will be equipped with everything you need to get your life together, find peace with yourself, and start progressing towards your ideal self.

I can give you this knowledge, but before diving in, you are probably wondering - why should I listen to you?

I'm not a scientist, or a world-famous expert in the field. I'm just a man with ADHD who lived most of his life in the shadows, undiagnosed and left to figure it out by himself.

I've dropped out of university degrees because of boredom and lack of motivation, lost promising career opportunities due to careless mistakes and impulsive decisions, and ruined countless relationships by snapping out of nowhere, forgetting something important, or failing to accept constructive criticism. My personal and career growth over the years has been an excruciatingly slow process of painful trial and error.

Before my diagnosis, I felt like there was something fundamentally and irreparably wrong with me.

If I had to label myself, my mind would inevitably drift toward phrases like "wasted potential," "not enough," "stupid," "lazy," and "below average." I was engulfed in shame for who I was and guilt for all my mistakes. I didn't even try to fight back on how horrible I felt because I thought the louder my inner demons were, the higher the chance for me to finally start listening and change.

I survived despite every setback, painful rejection, and gigantic failure. Now, I'm doing better than ever. However, I didn't get my life together because I finally whipped myself enough to get disciplined. Hating myself and being a workaholic didn't eventually pay off. Instead, getting my ADHD diagnosis was the turning point in my life.

Getting officially diagnosed offered me instant peace and clarity. Not because my life instantly improved but because I understood what was happening now. I could put my struggles and challenges into words. Getting this higher understanding of myself was cathartic because it absolved me from the guilt. I wasn't inherently broken anymore.

There was a clear reason why I was struggling so much. It felt like I finally stopped running, touched my back, and realized the heavy bag I had been carrying all along. Understanding the full context of my condition allowed me to tailor and customize every aspect of my life to be ADHD-friendly, and it began to get gradually better from this point onward.

I wouldn't have written this book if I had only my personal success to work with. However, the private coaching practice I have maintained for the past few years has shown me there are universally beneficial practices for neurodivergent people, regardless of age, career, background, family history, and other unique characteristics.

This book combines the experiences of hundreds of people in the hope of giving you clarity, momentum, and the necessary tools to navigate your ADHD. My only wish is to give you the wisdom and advice I wish I had received at the beginning of my journey.

If you tried everything and nothing has worked, then you've nothing to lose and everything to gain.

Take a leap of faith with me.

Chapter 1

What Is ADHD and How Does It Impact Men?

Having ADHD means the way you motivate yourself, manage emotions, concentrate, and stay productive will be very different compared to a neurotypical person. This is why the first task in building an ADHD-friendly habit, system, and life in general is to learn as much about your condition as possible.

This chapter will offer an in-depth explanation of ADHD, covering core definitions, common symptoms, statistics about the condition, outdated misconceptions, and how ADHD interacts with gender roles to create male-specific challenges.

Thinking of ADHD As a Problem To Be Solved Doesn't Work

Human beings are problem solvers. We are designed to survive and increase our chances of staying alive as much as possible by resolving any problems and challenges in our way. This problem-solving orientation is even more true for men. A gender differences study by M. Gallagher, R. De Lisi, and P. Holst has shown men as more goal-oriented problem solvers compared to women.[1]

In simpler terms, you are more likely to see what's in front of you as an obstacle to be overcome and a problem to be resolved. There is nothing wrong with this mindset in general. However, having ADHD is not a problem you can overcome traditionally. There is no quick fix, miraculous cure, or clear strategy to make it all disappear.

I'm sure you've already tried a lot to make it better. Cold showers, exercise, and a good diet so you can naturally produce more dopamine. Meditation and a rigid sleep schedule to improve cognitive function. Staying as healthy as possible makes symptoms less severe but doesn't remove them. It's an improvement but not a cure, which is why you may have the lingering feeling of not doing enough and not being enough.

How you feel about your progress is directly connected to the expectations you set for yourself. Imagine you've been running consistently for two months now, three times a week. If you expect to last 30 minutes per session without excessive fatigue and recover fairly quickly, you'll be happy with yourself. However, if you dream of being ready to run a marathon after three months, you are up for disappointment.

Similarly, how you feel about your progress with ADHD symptoms depends on your view of the condition. If you accept it as a permanent part of you, then simply reducing the intensity of your symptoms by 30% across the board is a huge victory. However, if you see it as a problem to be solved and removed from your to-do list, you will likely feel incompetent, incapable, and inadequate when you fall short of your unrealistic expectations.

This is one of the hardest beliefs to accept as a male with ADHD. From a young age, we are wired to believe we are all powerful, capable, and almighty. This perception is further developed by the media we consume. We see Navy seals, like David Goggins and Jocko Willink, achieve extreme discipline. Bodybuilders like Chris Bumstead and Arnold Schwarzenegger reach the full potential of the human body. Pioneers and innovators like Nikola Tesla and Richard Feynman started from nothing and climbed to the top.

It is imprinted in our heads time and time again that we can achieve anything, no matter how impossible and unreasonable it may appear at first. However, there are exceptions to everything.

There is nothing wrong with seeing them as role models and aspiring to be stronger, more resilient, mature, and stoic in your life. However, your effort, time, and energy should be going toward improving your symptoms, not trying to eliminate them. One is like swimming against the current - horribly exhausting and pointless, while the other is swimming with the current and learning to flow with the water - hard in the beginning but easier over time.

Just because you can't remove your ADHD doesn't mean you can't work on building habits, systems, and a lifestyle that is compatible with your conditions and helps you to reduce the negative impact of your symptoms. Life is not zero-sum. All or nothing. You can live a happy, productive, and meaningful life with ADHD, so stop trying to remove it and learn to live with it.

Your ADHD is not a curse or a superpower. It's not a problem to be solved or a blessing. Don't describe a negative or a positive value to it. Try to simply accept it the way it is.

If there were a rainstorm outside, you wouldn't curse the skies or express gratitude for the pouring clouds. You'd change your clothing and boots before going outside and get on with your day. Similarly, ADHD doesn't make you flawed, broken, or damaged. It's a part of yourself that can negatively affect your life, so you must embrace it and learn to work around it.

To accept your ADHD you must learn every single aspect of it. To manage the symptoms you must get to know them all and how they affect you. If you are ready to start working with your ADHD instead of against it, let's get started with the basics.

What Is ADHD?

ADHD is a genetic condition impacting the prefrontal cortex and other brain regions. It is a permanent and irreversible change in the brain, which can not be turned back or fixed. Contrary to outdated beliefs, ADHD is not a condition affecting only children, and many adults have been diagnosed as well.

ADHD doesn't only affect children, but in general, the symptoms appear very early into childhood. The exact cause of ADHD is yet to be determined, but genetics and environmental factors may play a role in increasing the risk of having ADHD.[2]

One certain risk factor is your family history. If one of your parents has ADHD, then the chance of having ADHD as well is much higher. Others include the mother's circumstances while carrying the child. According to some studies, smoking, consuming alcohol, being exposed to pesticides and other toxic chemical compounds, being born prematurely, with low weight, or suffering from a head injury can contribute to a higher risk.

Having ADHD means your brain structure and brain chemistry are different from other people. This is why you may stumble upon terms like neurodivergent, neuro-atypical, and other ways to describe people with ADHD and other neurodevelopmental conditions.

Symptoms of ADHD

The term ADHD stands for attention deficit hyperactivity disorder because the most common symptoms include inattention, hyperactivity, impulsivity, and other differences in how you think, behave, and experience the world. To be more specific:

1. **Inattention** - A struggle to regulate your attention, making you more likely to zone out, frequently lose concentration, and pay attention to details.

2. **Hyperactivity** - A constant feeling of restlessness, making you unable to sit still in one place for long. It can also be internal. Many people with ADHD feel bombarded with an overwhelming amount of thoughts on a daily basis. Rest comes only if you get an outlet, like physical activity or sharing your thoughts with people.

3. **Impulsivity** - An intense desire to follow impulses, intuition, and gut feelings without slowing down to think of the consequences. It can mean hasty purchases, poorly thought-out career changes, interrupting people in the middle of their speech, etc.

While the official diagnosis looks primarily at the big three, other officially recognized symptoms are worth noting. The changes in brain chemistry and structure lead to a cluster of other symptoms, which are broadly labeled as executive dysfunction. The negative impact of it can be so severe that some experts have suggested Executive Function Disorder as an alternative name for ADHD.

In short, your executive function is the cognitive ability and mental organization that allows you to pursue your goals. For you to reach your goals, you need to:

1. Analyze a task by comprehending its details and characteristics.
2. Devise a plan on how to address the task by thinking of how long it will take, how much effort it requires, and the order of steps that must be done to complete it.
3. Organize the steps in a way that works with your abilities and order them based on how big of a priority they are.
4. Adjust to any necessary changes and be able to juggle multiple pieces of information while doing the task or smoothly switch between interconnected tasks related to the overarching goal.
5. Practice self-restraint to control your impulses, avoid distractions, and stick to your goals.
6. Self-monitor effectively to see your progress and what's expected or required of you to reach your goals.

7. Pick and stick to timelines, which results in the goal being reached on time.

Ideally, executive function allows you to pick a task after analyzing the pros and cons and prioritizing the most important and urgent one. You'd also manage your time well, schedule accordingly, and complete it promptly while using willpower and discipline to stay on track and avoid distractions, temptations, and urges to give up altogether.

In reality, this perfect-looking sequence of events rarely happens when you start a work assignment, personal project or put your effort into anything else. On the contrary, you likely experience problems on multiple fronts whenever you try anything. This is because executive function issues lead to problems with control over thoughts, emotions, and behavior.

Those executive function problems look like the following ADHD symptoms:

1. **Impaired self-control** - You struggle to use willpower, stay disciplined, and power through when you don't enjoy what you are doing. Your brain is much more likely to prioritize upcoming deadlines and the closest sources of immediate stimulation at the expense of long-term gratification and decision-making.

2. **Differences in motivation** - Rewards in the future and the threat of punishment don't work for people with ADHD unless they are huge and severe or close in the future. Instead, the ADHD brain is driven by curiosity, excitement, variety, novelty, personal interest, and other sources of intrinsic motivation.

3. **Time blindness** - This is the inability to accurately assess what's the time. Time blindness means you struggle to estimate how much time a task will take and how to separate your time during the day.

4. **Forgetfulness** - Executive dysfunction often leads to working memory issues, meaning you struggle with short-term memories. The names of people, number sequences, dates, and other details may be forgotten seconds after you learn them.

5. **Mood swings** - Issues with self-control lead to problems when trying to keep emotions in check. Having ADHD increases the chance of intense emotions, sudden fluctuations between different emotional states, and the struggle to contain and compose yourself when hit with powerful emotions.

6. **Rejection Sensitivity Dysphoria** - This symptom doesn't have sufficient clinical evidence to make it official, but leading experts, like Dr. William Dodson, speculate it's part of ADHD. RSD means you are more likely to see criticism and constructive feedback as personal attacks and interpret neutral situations as rejection from others.[3]

Extensive research has been done across the decades, and there is a clear connection between ADHD symptoms and their negative impact on the standard of living.

Some of the most obvious dangers you should be aware of include the following:

ADHD often correlates with other mental disorders

A meta-analysis of multiple ADHD studies by doctor Martin A. Katzman and his colleagues have shown a consistent pattern of ADHD leading to an increased chance of also being diagnosed with anxiety, bipolar, and other mood disorders. One study, in particular, done by Katzman and Sternat, showed how 34% of people with treatment-resistant depression were actually suffering from ADHD. The additional stress, fatigue, and low self-worth coming from ADHD all increase your risk of other mental health disorders.[4]

ADHD increases the chance for substance abuse

The constant craving for stimulation and the torture of chronic boredom push many people with ADHD towards substance abuse in a dire bid for pleasure, thrill, and novelty. A meta-analysis by Courtney A. Zulauf, Susan E. Sprich, and Steven A. Safren saw a recurring connection between young adults who were going through cannabis, tobacco, cocaine, alcohol, and other kinds of substance abuse treatment programs and an already established or subsequently discovered diagnosis with ADHD. Although the exact percentage varies, studies decisively show people with ADHD are at a higher risk of developing a substance abuse disorder.[5]

ADHD makes you more likely to experience difficulties in your professional life

You have likely experienced this yourself. Inability to concentrate, lack of attention to detail, careless mistakes, poor time management, and chronic procrastination make you less likely to obtain and maintain employment. Having a condition makes you a more risky hire with a competitive disadvantage compared to other candidates.[6]

ADHD makes maintaining personal connections much harder

Living together with a person who often forgets, stays disorganized, and struggles with home tasks is a very common source of constant fighting. Furthermore, impulsivity and issues with emotional control can increase the chance for immature slip-ups, petty infighting, and escalation of conflict with your significant other, friends, and family.

ADHD is no joke. This is why it is considered a mental health disorder and disability by many governments, and an official diagnosis comes with support from public bodies and an expectation for appropriate accommodation by companies.

ADHD Types

If you have been diagnosed with ADHD, you will have most or all symptoms present. However, the frequency and intensity of each symptom will depend on the type of ADHD you have. Currently, the DSM-5 breaks down ADHD into three subtypes: inattentive, hyperactive-impulsive, or combination.

Inattentive

If you are predominantly inattentive, you will likely be disorganized, easily distracted, and face immense difficulty getting motivated to do specific tasks. You could be zoning out in the middle of a conversation, daydreaming when you should be doing work, or trying to simultaneously process multiple things in your mind. Your mind is likely erratic and full of chaos.

Sustaining attention on tasks is often very daunting, especially when they are not interesting or engaging. You can still be productive and finish your work on time, but it will require three times the effort because you must constantly force and supervise yourself. Work often leaves you exhausted, and even with the best effort, you still miss some details and make careless mistakes.

Boys and men with inattentiveness are the hardest to detect because the symptoms are invisible. With hyperactive combined, you can feel the intense energy around the child and see them constantly fidgeting and moving around. However, inattentive types slip under the radar because they don't cause that much trouble or bring so much attention to themselves.

This is the child who says little and seems stuck in their internal world, which leaves the parents to think of them as shy and introverted. The boy gazing out of the window during class often forgets to do his homework and is seen as lazy and lacking talent. The man who doesn't jump around and cause a commotion but their hundreds of racing thoughts leave them chronically stressed, which leads to skin picking, nail-biting, teeth grinding, and foot tapping as a way to channel the energy outside.

Hyperactive

The predominantly hyperactive-impulsive types are usually the kids who get diagnosed first. These are the stereotypical features of ADHD that are more visible. You still may experience similar symptoms regarding disorganization and distraction, but not to the same degree.

Instead, you are more likely to feel restless, fidgety, and unable to stay still. You could be known as a person who talks excessively; some may even call you intense because of how animated or excited you get. Your brain is like a race car without the breaks, constantly having the urge to be on the move and doing something, which makes you more impulsive. You act before you think or blurt things out before it's your turn. Actions just happen before you know it, and you are left to deal with the consequences.

Combined

If you have a combined presentation, you have characteristics of inattentive and hyperactive presentations. They combine into one seemingly contradictory but very much real condition. How your symptoms manifest will depend on your environment, current mood, and recent events.

One moment, you may be passively listening in the background of a group setting, and the other, you hijack the conversation with four sudden interruptions and feel an intense urge to mention something vaguely related to the topic. One day, you feel highly energized in an almost manic episode of motivation, but the next day, you feel lethargic, irritable, and stressed.

How Rare Is ADHD?

Many men who've been diagnosed in childhood, who recently went through the bumpy road of getting an adult diagnosis, or who suspect they may have ADHD tend to gaslight themselves with numbers to convince themselves they are "normal" and "ordinary."

You know very well what society expects out of a man. This looks like your dad's cold remarks to get up and stop crying after falling off the bike. The look of disgust and pity you get from girls if they see you complaining or expressing your insecurities and emotions. Even from those closest to us with good intentions, we are often expected to be stoic, solid, and always strong.

We feel a strong need to conform, not to be different. To be strong, not handicapped, disabled, and troubled in any way. This masculine spirit is what often leads us to question an ADHD diagnosis, even after official testing. The easiest way to put doubt is to justify it with numbers. If it affects a very small percentage of the population, then it's not likely we are the exception, right?

Not quite. The truth is far from the intuition you may already have.

The current data on how many people have ADHD is not conclusive. Some estimates show that between 6 to 9% of US children have ADHD, and the worldwide number of ADHD cases sits at around 5%.[5] Other studies suggest around 8.7% of children in the US have been diagnosed with ADHD, and the worldwide population of neurodivergent people can go up to 6.7% for adults.[7] No matter the exact numbers you are looking at, the results are significant.

This is official data only for people officially diagnosed and registered in governmental and private records. There are many other people who refuse to seek out help due to distrust in the system, lack of awareness of their symptoms as caused by ADHD, lack of time and money to spare towards diagnosis and treatment, or a total lack of institutional support for mental health disorders.

If all those exceptions were not long enough, there are a few more. Some people do get diagnosed but don't get treated for the root cause of their symptoms - ADHD. Instead, they get diagnosed with anxiety, depression, OCD, and other disorders. Some medical professionals falsely believe ADHD is over-diagnosed. The condition can only affect children, so adults don't have it or buy into the fear-mongering around stimulants and may be reluctant and refuse to diagnose people who have the symptoms.

In sum, the official percentage is high enough, but it is very likely an even larger number of people have ADHD but continue to live in the shadows without a diagnosis. ADHD is far more common than many people think, which is why, in recent years, as mental health awareness and support become mainstream, the rate of diagnosis has jumped significantly.

Instead of thinking of yourself as a cursed exception, it's much more helpful and less shameful to see yourself as one of many people who are simply different. Personally, knowing just how many people are going through the same is highly reassuring. If they can succeed, so can you. You are not alone in this fight.

Myths About ADHD

Now you know ADHD is not just some fringe condition affecting a tiny percent of the population. However, there are many other mainstream misconceptions, myths, and lies about ADHD, which need to be addressed for you to have an accurate picture of the condition.

The reasons for those ADHD myths are many. Most obviously, the research field for ADHD is incomplete, and there are many disputes between different theories. Outside of academics, there is a lot of prejudice against mental health disorders. Since they are not visible, people dismiss them altogether or minimize how painful they are. Unfortunately, for many people, it's easier to attack with prejudice and stick negative labels (lazy, undisciplined, irresponsible, etc) to people who struggle instead of offering empathy and understanding.

Furthermore, many people struggle to fully grasp what you are going through (empathy gap), so they assume it's not so severe if they have experienced similar symptoms at some point - lack of motivation, procrastination, issues with time management, etc. Although all people have such experiences, it's obvious how having ADHD makes the symptoms much more severe.

Let's go through the most common myths one by one.

Myth I - ADHD Is Just An Excuse: You Are Lazy And Stupid So Try Harder

We live in a highly individualistic society; you are solely responsible for yourself, so if there is a problem in your life, it must be a personal failure. This is why expressing your struggle with ADHD is often met with a mix of negative reactions, from skepticism to dismissal and disgust at showing weakness.

If you've ever fallen behind, failed to meet the standards and expectations of others, or failed in anything, you've likely been called lazy, irresponsible, incompetent, stupid, or any other negative label. Ignoring how offensive such remarks are for a moment, they are not based on reality. All those labels imply you have a choice - you could work, but instead, you procrastinate on your phone. The fact you choose the wrong option is the problem.

However, having ADHD is not a choice, and the symptoms you experience are not a switch you can quickly turn on and off for your convenience. Executive dysfunction makes it much more likely to experience paralysis, mental blocks, forgetfulness, issues staying motivated, and distractibility while trying to work. None of those challenges are choices you willingly make.[8]

A lazy person prefers to spend their time pursuing leisure and pleasure and chooses not to expend their energy on work. An irresponsible person sees their careless mistakes but does not care enough to correct them and be better in the future. I am sure you are not that kind of person. You have goals, priorities, and dreams and are trying to better yourself, but the cards you were dealt make it difficult. It's not a question of desire but of the ability to make this desire into reality.

This is why the notion of being stupid and intellectually inferior with ADHD is absurd. You know what needs to be done, but your brain struggles to turn this intention into action. This is an executive function deficit. Having ADHD is like being a passenger in a car driving in the wrong direction. You know where you are going is wrong, but you feel powerless to change direction.

Picture yourself as the CEO in an important meeting, and the executive function is your secretary, whose responsibility is to help keep you on task. The problem isn't your lack of qualifications and expertise.

Rather, it's your secretary not doing their job and allowing everybody who wants to barge into your office unannounced. You can still get some work done, but it would be much easier if somebody weren't constantly interrupting your workflow.

Just like a company can have the most talented employees but struggle without a manager to coordinate and supervise the whole process, you are highly intelligent and capable but struggle to realize this potential because of executive dysfunction.

Myth II - ADHD Is a Disorder Only for Children Because Adults Grow Out of It

In early research, scientists focused on hyperactivity as the hallmark of the condition and noticed that these issues weren't as prominent as children hit puberty.

This led to the belief that ADHD is a condition exclusive to children, and with age, symptoms would become less severe and eventually stop. The natural development of the brain, especially the prefrontal cortex responsible for focus and impulse control, would eventually end up by 25, and then you are fixed.

Later findings revealed that some symptoms may appear less severe, not because they disappear, but because they become less visible due to improved coping mechanisms. Being externally hyperactive as a child turns into anxiety and racing thoughts as an adult. Impulsiveness is less obvious because you learn to keep your mouth shut at work but still make impulsive purchases and personal decisions.

Naturally, as you grow older, you become better at masking and coping with your symptoms. However, this doesn't mean your ADHD is cured or the struggle has ended. For instance, just because you have a convoluted productivity system with 37 reminders in your calendar and a personalized to-do list doesn't mean tasks still don't take three times more effort. You've just reduced the chaos with organizational skills, but the mental exhaustion and stress remain.

Myth III - You Are Supposed To Be Hyperactive and Impulsive If You Really Have ADHD

This myth plays into the caricature of a child recklessly running around, yelling, and being led solely by their impulses. While it is certainly one component of ADHD, it's not right to associate ADHD solely with hyperactivity just because it's the most visible and loud symptom that can be spotted.

Many children with ADHD miss a diagnosis because they have a different subtype of the condition - inattentive ADHD. They miss assignments, forget important events, zone out during conversations, and struggle to articulate themselves. Unfortunately, it's easy enough for people to dismiss those issues as personal failings instead of seeing them as signs of a larger problem.

Many young boys who grow into men internalize masculine ideals, like being stoic, actively suppressing and avoiding emotional talk, and staying calm and composed no matter what. If you fall into this group, then you have ADHD, but it looks different because you can self-regulate, mask your symptoms, or deal with issues that are not obvious to the eye - anxiety, procrastination, fleeting attention, addiction, etc.

The Science of Your Brain – How ADHD Works

The root cause of ADHD is impairment in the optimal growth and development of the brain.

Some theories suggest brain regions, like the prefrontal cortex, don't develop as quickly and remain smaller even after full growth. Other theories focus on communication between brain regions and suggest that the chemicals designed to facilitate this connection (neurotransmitters) may not work properly.[9]

Much of the research around ADHD has so far centered around impairments in the prefrontal cortex because it is the region responsible for many of the tasks people with ADHD struggle with - time management, organization, self-control, working memory, motivation, emotional control, etc. One of the easiest ways of understanding how the prefrontal cortex works is by following Doctor Berkley's four-components model.[10]

Doctor Russell Berkley, one of the pioneers in ADHD research and treatment, has systemized the prefrontal cortex as one consisting of four circuits: The "What," "When," "Why," and "Who" circuits of the prefrontal cortex. To be more specific:

1. **The "What" circuit** - This circuit is related to working memory, which is the limited amount of short-term information you have available to aid any cognitive process that is useful in the present. Those can include focusing on a single task, remembering and following up on instructions with multiple layers and sets of information, planning for the future, etc. People with ADHD experience problems with working memory, which impair their ability to prioritize, keep multiple ideas in mind simultaneously, and plan a multi-step approach to their actions.

2. **The "When" circuit** - This circuit is responsible for the timing, time management, and perception of time. Disruptions in the "When" circuit can lead to a distorted perception of time passing and affect the ability to plan things in order. This is why people with ADHD submit assignments late, struggle to arrive on time for appointments, or completely forget and lose track of time.

3. **The "Why" circuit** - This is the circuit making the final decisions. It is connected to your emotions, and it weighs how you feel with the logical aspects of the decision. Impairments in this circuit due to ADHD can make you more impulsive and less considerate of the pros and cons of a decision and the potential long-term impacts.

4. **The "Who" circuit** - This circuit is responsible for self-awareness. It considers what you are doing and your ability to recognize your feelings externally and internally. If you've ever spent a few hours on social media in a zombified state with no awareness of what happened, struggled

to express how you are feeling, or smashed into a wall or a door because you weren't aware of them, it was an issue with this circuit.

The structural changes in the brain of a person with ADHD are only half of the picture. The other part has to do with neurotransmitters - the brain's messengers responsible for sending signals from one brain circuit to the other. Many theories suggest people with ADHD don't produce enough neurotransmitters, or the receptors in the brain are not responsive to them.

If you've ever heard dopamine mentioned in the same context as ADHD (dopamine starved, craving dopamine, naturally producing dopamine, etc), now you know why. Dopamine, along with acetylcholine, norepinephrine, serotonin, and gamma-aminobutyric acid (GABA), are the primary neurotransmitters of the brain.

Dopamine is associated with excitement, desire, and cravings for more. Most importantly, dopamine is what gives you the motivation to pursue anything in life. Dopamine makes you look towards the future for something valuable, exciting, and novel and pushes you to acquire it.

The "molecule of desire" changes your cognitive abilities by improving your focus and alertness to what is happening around you. If you stop to think for a moment, it makes total sense. If you crave something, you naturally want to be alert to the external world and mentally sharp to acquire it. Dopamine is a messenger between circuits in the brain, activating them whenever appropriate to complete the necessary task.

Dopamine production sees a massive boost when we crave something or anticipate a desirable future event. Even without such stimulation, your body steadily produces dopamine throughout the day to aid in movement, cognitive tasks, and anything that requires motivation.

There are many theories surrounding this crucial neurotransmitter - dopamine production is reduced, the molecules are metabolized much more quickly, the receptors in the brain are simply not responsible for dopamine, etc. No matter the explanation, the result is all the same. If you have ADHD, you are dopamine deficient, and what you produce is not enough to always meet your needs.

Connecting this dopamine deficiency to your ADHD symptoms begins to tie it all together.

The most popular medicines for ADHD, approved by scientific research, are stimulants precisely because they fill in for what you are not producing to a sufficient degree - neurotransmitters like dopamine and norepinephrine. This is also why stimulants can reduce symptoms. The higher dopamine production improves messaging to the prefrontal cortex, allowing it to work optimally.

Without medication or other natural ways to produce enough dopamine, the brain compensates by changing your behavior.

Impulsiveness, hyper-focus on interests and projects, cravings for stimulation, and intrinsically motivating experiences make a lot more sense if you know you are dopamine deficient. Your brain is a starving man, and it'd prefer immediate relief because the lack of sufficient neurotransmitters makes it dismiss and de-prioritize the future.

Chapter 2

Discover Self-Confidence and Overcome the Stigma of ADHD

Having ADHD can feel like a curse mark. Saying it casually can lead to accusations of making excuses just to get stimulants. Mentioning it to a recruiter or during an interview can put you on the blacklist of candidates who'd be a good fit but would require too much investment and accommodation. Sharing it with a partner may not lead to the understanding you hoped for and may be seen as an excuse.

This chapter will offer a comprehensive look into the stigma many men with ADHD experience from loved ones, co-workers, strangers, and society in general. After exploring the problem, we will offer ways to cultivate acceptance and reduce negative self-talk with simple and science-based exercises you can easily do in your everyday life.

The Stigma Of ADHD and Its Impact on Self-Confidence

ADHD has been around for centuries, if not since the beginning of the human species. However, the first empirical observations of the condition began in the early 20th century, and it was officially recognized as a mental health disorder in the 1960s. Even if it has gradually entered the mainstream, many people still treat the condition with skepticism or denial.

If you mention symptoms, like lack of attention control, you are likely to start an intense exchange on how smartphones, the internet, and social media, in particular, have zombified society, and you should cut them off if you want to focus better. Saying you have intense and often uncontrollable impulses and can't sit still is met with phrases like "boys will be boys" and "you just need to exercise more."

Does life feel dull and mundane to the point of throwing you into panic or a depressive episode?

Prepare to hear your parents or friends dismiss your experience by saying life is boring most of the time, and you should just get used to it.

Stigma against ADHD ranges from trivialization of the symptoms to rejection of the condition as real. At the root of it all is the often unbreachable empathy gap - people struggle to understand the feelings, thoughts, and experiences of others because they use themselves as a reference, even if they are vastly different as people. If a neurotypical person sometimes forgets, procrastinates from time to time, and doesn't always feel motivated, then they falsely assume those experiences can't be so fatal and deliberating since they manage to overcome them in the end.

There is also stigmatization related to the most common ADHD treatments. If you seek a diagnosis and mention you went through the effort of getting officially tested, very often, the response would subtly or even quite directly accuse you of looking for the easy way out with drugs. Many people feel strong negative feelings about stimulants and voice out their prejudice by calling you a junkie or an addict if you are on medication.

The paradox of stigma against ADHD is you end up feeling horrible no matter what people think. Some people accept your condition only to start treating you as a borderline destructive, dysfunctional, and disruptive liability. Others minimize and deny your diagnosis and suffering, leaving you to question the severity of your symptoms and gaslight yourself that you should try harder and they may be right.

If self-confidence comes from reaching a sense of harmony with yourself, security in your competence and use for others, and approval and support by the people around you, then the stigma around ADHD often clashes with all of them. This is why many therapists and mental health experts speak interchangeably about having ADHD and low self-worth. The connection is so strong that you'd need a miracle not to feel insecure and unworthy in at least something with ADHD.

Accepting ADHD and Yourself

Have you ever read cheesy advice about positive affirmations, embracing authenticity, and the need to love yourself for who you are? According to this optimistic viewpoint, life would be better if you love your personality, quirks, and how your brain works.

Years ago, I'd constantly stumble on such recommendations. Honestly, it made me want to vomit. There wasn't anything fundamentally wrong with this advice, but I felt so repulsed and disgusted by the idea because I wasn't in the right headspace to accept it.

See, the way you view yourself is a spectrum. If you are into numbers, think of it as 0 to 100. At the very bottom, you loathe every aspect of your existence. The more you climb, the more your hatred becomes ambivalence, acceptance, tolerance, and eventually liking and even love. Someone telling you to love yourself sounds absurd and even offensive if you are near the bottom.

This is why you need to start with acceptance before you can even think of liking and loving yourself.

But what does it mean to accept? It's easier to define what it is not. Acceptance is not a one-time magical ritual where you find the strength to utter some holy words only to be flooded with a feeling of catharsis and relief. It's also not a snap of your fingers where you suddenly get a life-changing epiphany and begin to see yourself and the world differently.

Self-acceptance means embracing every aspect of your ADHD, personality, and who you are as a person without trying to fundamentally alter and change them. It is about accepting the set of cards you've been dealt with and playing them to the best of your abilities instead of desperately trying to get a redraw.

On paper, it sounds very simple and easy to follow, but embracing who you are is one of the hardest parts of having ADHD. People struggle with self-acceptance because they still wish to entirely change parts of themselves. You can't accept being forgetful if you think forgetfulness is a sign of low intellect and you wish to be better than that. Nor can you accept how your energy and motivation fluctuate if you desire to be highly disciplined and consistent with your routine.

While self-acceptance is a concession that there are limits to who you can be, it doesn't mean you completely surrender and give up. Many men struggle with self-acceptance because they associate it with defeat. They think that if you can't change yourself to the core, then you are bound to remain mediocre and unfulfilled for the rest of your life. This couldn't be further from the truth.

Let's take one of the most common ADHD challenges - working memory. I'm sure you've forgotten appointments, upcoming birthdays, special anniversaries, and other important dates, events, and memories.

Trying to force yourself to remember, using memorization techniques, and practicing a few times a week could lead to some improvements, and it is a worthwhile goal. However, it'd be much easier if you truly accept this is a permanent feature of who you are and work around that. For instance, your effort and energy could be spent more productively if you just relied more on systems, like calendars, alarms, and reminders, so you don't have to stress yourself so much to remember and keep everything in your mind all the time.

Ultimately, self-acceptance is about drawing the line between what you can't control at all, what you can partially influence, and what is within your full control. For instance, you can not remove or change your ADHD. It is a permanent, and irreversible part of who you are and how you feel, think, and behave. However, you have room to improve your symptoms and make them better with lifestyle changes, therapy, and finding the right environment and system.

This looks like synching your alarms with your calendar and other documents, apps, and software to stay on top of upcoming assignments, events, and tasks instead of stubbornly relying on your memory and blaming yourself when you forget.

Working to improve your diet and being content with the improvement in alertness and energy levels instead of drowning in supplements and obsessing over the optimal pill stack you can get to somehow cure your brain chemistry. Putting a cap on phone use and not taking any devices when out for a walk, but not trying a bold dopamine detox where you cut any ounce of pleasure and enjoyment from your life until you snap.

Acceptance doesn't have to be overly complicated. You can intentionally reflect, journal, and write about the aspects of yourself you struggle to accept. This can help you to pinpoint what keeps you dissatisfied and frustrated, giving you the clarity needed to decide if it can be completely changed, or if you just need to accept it and work around it. More than a daily practice, many of your actions can take you closer to self-acceptance.

For instance, making a quick improvised meal, like microwaved oatmeal, a protein smoothie, or a basic sandwich, instead of thinking it's either a full meal or nothing shows you accept how you won't always feel well enough to have perfect nutrition. Similarly, taking the bold step to change careers for a more dynamic environment packed with variety and stimulation shows you accept how the repetitive and mundane corporate grind isn't ADHD-friendly in any way for you.

Your brain works on repetition. If, in the past, all your words, behavior, and actions did was work against you instead of working with you, then reversing course will take some time. The road toward self-acceptance is turbulent, and full of setbacks and regressions. It's neither smooth nor instant. However, with every step, you get closer to feeling okay in your own skin.

Accepting Yourself Despite What Others and Society Say

So far, we have talked about acceptance as an internal fight with yourself. You battled parts of yourself as if they were demons that could be purified and destroyed with enough effort, hard work, and sacrifice. Once you learn to befriend them and work together, life becomes much easier because you don't live every day with an intense feeling of inadequacy and shame.

However, sometimes, the real demons hurting your ability to accept yourself are the people around you. Even if your inner critic is loud and persistent, once you tame it, you may realize many other voices are making you feel flawed, imperfect, and broken. It hurts even more when they come from friends, family, and colleagues.

Practicing self-acceptance can be very challenging, if not impossible, if you are in a toxic social environment. A career change in a more ADHD-friendly direction can be met with disappointed snarking from your father, who expected you to toughen up and accept life isn't easy. Taking your available paid leave to avoid burnout may be ridiculed by colleagues who say survival of the fittest is already showing its first victims.

If a person is continuously toxic towards you and keeps tanking your confidence and sense of self-worth without any reasoning or justification, then the most straightforward solution is to cut them from your life. For instance, if it's a friend, stop hanging out with them or texting them, and when they try to initiate anything, either be blunt with them or do the bare minimum, so they get the message.

Cutting off sounds good on paper, but in real life, it very often doesn't work. You can't stop your colleagues from blabbering because you are not in a position to change jobs, and HR conforms to a workaholic culture in the workplace. Your father may have been an asshole about it, but you still need his financial assistance to make ends meet, and most of the time, you get along rather well.

People aren't evil creatures who exist to torment you. Sometimes, confronting them about it is enough to set the record straight and get them to stop ruining your confidence. It is not comfortable at all to potentially start a fight or conflict with the other person, but passive suffering in silence isn't pleasant either. In the best case, they will realize the comments were insensitive, while in the worst, they will stubbornly retain their position. They prefer to keep your friendship and professional relationship intact, so they will shut up about it.

This is not a perfect solution, but real life is not a mathematical equation where you can take steps X, Y, and Z to find yourself in an optimal social environment. Sometimes, when nothing else works, you just shrug it off and move on. Words can get to you if you let them. Although you can't entirely stop the visceral reaction you feel to what others say, over time, you can learn to change how you respond.

Remind yourself how they don't know who you are, what you have been through, and the full context of your situation, so their thoughts are meaningless. Just like we get all sorts of intrusive thoughts during the day and don't follow up on them, you also don't have to accept or let yourself be influenced by what others say about you.

Now, it is worth stressing that shrugging it off doesn't mean sucking it up in silence and bottling it up in yourself. If it wouldn't hurt you, confronting them and expressing your discomfort, offense, and disgust with their words is worth it simply to express how you feel about their derogatory remarks.

If it's not possible, say it is coming from your manager, boss, or a parent on whom you are financially dependent, you can always find an outlet with friends and other loved ones to express your dissatisfaction. Having an outlet is essential because simply taking the punches without any response makes it more likely for you to think they may be right in some way.

Balancing Compassion and Forgiveness With Self-Responsibility

Even if you want to accept yourself and feel ready to break free from social pressure and expectations, you may find yourself reluctant to take the step. Very often, men feel as though accepting their ADHD means stopping the fight, and this clashes with their sense of responsibility to always do as much as possible.

After all, many people draw the difference between a boy and a man based on their self-responsibility. Finding excuses or putting the blame on others is always easier, which is why seeing yourself as fully responsible for your actions and their consequences is a clear sign of maturity. Trying to find the fault in anyone but yourself is a sign of weakness, making you less of a man.

For most men, this is common sense and the rule by which they try to design their responses to everything. But what happens when you really don't have control over specific circumstances, like your ADHD diagnosis? What kind of responsibility do you have, then?

When the topic of responsibility comes up in the ADHD community, the stance taken is often one of trying to validate your experiences and emotions. It goes something like this:

ADHD is a mental health disorder that seriously affects multiple aspects of your brain responsible for keeping you disciplined, motivated, and productive. If you struggle, this is normal. Just because you feel behind doesn't mean there is anything inherently flawed, broken, and damaged about you. It is normal because your ADHD brain is at odds with the way our society is constructed.

You crave physical activity and a dynamic and ever-changing environment, but you are forced to work in a sedentary workplace with a mundane and repetitive routine. You crave stimulation, variety, and excitement, but life encourages you to settle down, specialize in a niche, and stay structured. Even if you can contain your impulses, personalized ads, invasive content, and manipulative marketing strategies all seek to take advantage of your impulsivity.

It's the design and expectations of society that often cause pain and stress.

This is true, and you know it. We all have an inner critic who pushes us to try harder and keep going no matter what. But reading and contemplating reminders like this are essential because they urge us to have some compassion for ourselves. After all, the inner critic is useful only if it keeps you accountable and motivated, not when it crushes your ego and demotivates you to a point where you feel it's no longer worth trying anything because you are bound to fail.

Okay, point taken. Your actions are not a personal failure. Struggle doesn't equal you being lazy, stupid, or incompetent. And you deserve a pat on the back for pulling through despite everything, especially if you've recently been diagnosed as an adult since you had to figure it all out on your own. Acknowledging this can feel liberating and cathartic because there is less reason to be ashamed if the fault doesn't entirely lie with you.

This sounds good on paper, but I am sure you have some resistance while reading this. An uncomfortable and icky feeling you can't shake off. Maybe you were a bit too harsh on yourself, but what comes after treating yourself with compassion and forgiveness?

Isn't feeling radically responsible for everything the only way to get anything done?

After all, being responsible for everything is draining and mentally exhausting, but it gives you a sense of freedom, right? You may not always do the right thing, but you feel in control because it creates a perception of choice. It's fine to sometimes make the wrong choice because this means you retain your freedom. If you consciously make a wrong choice, you can consciously make a good one as well.

Whenever I get stuck in this dilemma about compassion and responsibility, I like to remind myself that it's not all or nothing. They are not mutually exclusive - you can have them both. If responsibility is like a collar on your neck, keeping you in line, all you have to do is reduce the tension a bit to free up breathing space. Treating yourself with kindness doesn't mean you abandon all sense of responsibility.

You can acknowledge how having ADHD is out of your control and how certain symptoms will lead to behavior that is unavoidable and inevitable - feeling demotivated and drained of energy on certain days, making impulsive remarks to a friend, or struggling with assignments requiring lots of working memory. However, you should still take responsibility for the consequences and try to be better in the future.

If you interrupt a friend during a conversation and make immature remarks, apologize and make an effort not to interrupt so suddenly next time. If you impulsively purchase tons of items for a new passion without consulting your partner, say you are sorry and commit to putting a lower cap on your credit card so you can't purchase above budget in seconds. When you forget someone's birthday, don't beat yourself up over it, but wish them a happy birthday, even if it's three days later, and set a reminder in your calendar for the next time.

Mistakes will often happen. This is part of being human. Forgive yourself, show some kindness, and understand in the same way you'd treat a close friend who failed in something. Then, channel your drive to be better and control your life by making sure it doesn't repeat as often or to the same degree in the future.

Acceptance Doesn't Happen Alone – Overcoming Isolation and Refusal To Get Help From Others

When you think of masculinity, you think of independence, self-reliance, solitude, and individualism. You are told that as a man, you are strong because you can figure it out by yourself. You are not only powerful enough to manage independently, but it is also your duty. To sacrifice yourself and be the protector of others, and not a burden and waste to society.

There are countless stories, media portrayals, and narratives of legendary men who overcame unimaginable obstacles alone. We've all heard the stories of boat crash survivors who stayed alive for weeks at sea, people born without limbs who didn't give up despite their disability, and veterans who had survived horrifying traumas while on duty.

Self-reliance makes sense on paper. People will not always be around, but you always have yourself. You also don't want to bother others too much because they also have their own problems, challenges, and responsibilities. It's a matter of pride as well. It feels good to hold a badge of independence on your chest. While independence is often desirable, taking it to the extreme is problematic.

It feels good to frame your solitude as independence, but sometimes the truth is we are struggling with loneliness and seek excuses to justify it. After all, being by yourself because you are career-focused and not currently focusing on relationships sounds much better than admitting you feel an overwhelming sense of shame and guilt. Emotions are so intense that they urge you to push others away in fear of loved ones seeing your flaws, imperfections, and shortcomings.

Low self-worth and chronic feelings of shame and inadequacy often accompany ADHD. You fail to meet your standards or those of society, making you feel ashamed of yourself and not enough. You don't want others to see this side of you, so you push them away, make excuses, and rationalize your loneliness with pragmatic reasons.

Unfortunately, the more you stay alone, the worse it gets. How you feel about yourself is a game of comparison. Humans were designed to compare with others and to feel envy, jealousy, and other nasty emotions, which are not pleasant at all but very motivating to get your act together.

If you have close people around you, it's natural to have candid conversations and moments of vulnerability from time to time. It's reassuring in a way. You are not perfect, but neither are they. If you are broken, then all of you are broken together. But, once you begin to isolate yourself, this feeling of solidarity and comradery disappears. It starts to feel like everyone else is doing great, and you are the only failure who's falling behind.

We are designed as social creatures who crave deep and meaningful connections, which is why I'm sure this is very likely to apply to you. Still, maybe the discomfort from loneliness is painful but not enough to convince you to abandon your pride in self-reliance. If that's the case, I have one more trick up my sleeve, and it begins with a simple question.

Is it reasonable for businesses to outsource?

Of course. If you were a marketing agency, trying to do your accounting by yourself and assigning it to your employees would be a disaster. A similar situation would arise if a new technology existed on the market, like generative AI. You could ask your employees to spend time learning about it, but it's more reasonable to get specialized consultants to do some internal training.

We don't expect businesses, creating millions or even billions of profit each year, to be perfect entities capable of handling every situation and holding expertise in every domain. It's natural to focus on your strengths and outsource your weaknesses, right?

If this logic applies to multi-billion businesses, I'm not sure why it shouldn't apply to you as well.

If you struggle to get out of bed and go to the gym constantly, there's nothing wrong with asking a friend to work out together so you stay accountable. It's okay to accept a group study session when you can't study because being with others creates pressure to study. If you are a busy entrepreneur, it's not a sign of weakness to get a virtual assistant to address your ADHD-specific problems, like forgetfulness and disorganization.

If this doesn't sound like common sense, let me blow your mind even further - you are already doing it. When you are seriously sick, you go to the doctor. When you have a legal issue, you contact a lawyer. If the car breaks down completely, you contact a mechanic. If relying on others is acceptable professionally, why should it differ from personal situations?

Sure, you are bothering them a bit, but if you have a loving partner, caring family, and loyal friends, they wouldn't mind. After all, you implicitly agree to be by their side if they have issues as well, right? Self-reliance is often a pragmatic choice, but sometimes, you must step back and reflect on whether you are being independent with a good reason or hopelessly stubborn.

This is especially true for getting help for your ADHD. Reading this book is a good first step, and I am sure you will make lots of progress on your own, but it's always easier if you have options to rely upon. A therapist to deal with pent-up emotions and create action plans, a coach to keep you accountable and work on your career and personal growth, or even local and online communities if you don't have the money to spare for professional help. There are many options, each of which can be immensely helpful.

Previously, we discussed balancing compassion and kindness with responsibility because it's not zero-sum. Similarly, relying on others is not an all-or-nothing situation. Going to therapy once a week, hanging around in online communities with other ADHD-ers, and making an effort to spend time with friends is not a slippery slope towards becoming dependent on others and getting weak. It's quite the opposite.

Cultivating Unshakeable Self-Esteem

When we think of confident people, it is easiest to connect self-esteem with fame and success. Most famous and accomplished people appear to beam with confidence, and even if they are more humble, there is a silent air of self-assurance around them. After all, it is easy to have confidence in yourself if you are an expert in a field, with multiple trophies and reminders of your accomplishments and many people looking for your guidance and expertise.

Here is the cold truth - building unshakeable self-esteem will happen only when your effort, commitment, and sacrifice lead to tangible results, a shift in your day-to-day actions, mindsets, and undeniable competency in a field. You don't build confidence through illusions but by growing into a person who masters their body, mind, and spirit and becomes useful to their loved ones, community, and society in general.

Self-talk, mantras, and other odd techniques for an instant confidence boost don't work for most men because we don't like BS. We know it is fake and not based on reality. Real self-esteem takes months, years, or even decades to build with grit, patience, and persistence. On the one hand, this is disappointing because if you feel low right now, there is no immediate relief. But, on the other hand, it is reassuring because once you get the ball rolling, it is much easier to keep and make your sense of self-esteem even stronger.

If you've done competitive swimming for five years as a teen, it is much easier to get into the gym and feel confident you will get results. If you've got a job once while feeling underqualified, it gives you the bravery to try again when you want to find a better-paying position. This can work even if the connection is not direct. Surviving a challenging four-year degree doesn't mean you will thrive at work, but it gives you enough confidence because you are used to dealing with on-the-spot thinking, tight deadlines, and a huge workload.

All you need is a single anchor you can return to whenever you get filled with doubt, anxiety, and other insecurities. If you have done it once, you can do it again, even if it's in a radically different field and subject. After all, no matter what you are doing, you need the same skills - critical thinking, willingness to accept and learn from mistakes, persistence and commitment, and others.

But what if you are at the very bottom right now with nothing to pull you upward?

Many people find themselves feeling incompetent, worthless, useless, and lacking in any significance. You can always get it together and get the ball rolling if you have some foundation to fall back on, an anchor to use as a confidence boost, but what if you have nothing?

Even if you don't believe in yourself, I believe in you.

We are designed to focus on the negative. It is in our biological nature to dwell on what we lack, what could be better, and what is missing. The primal instincts driving us all focus on survival, accomplishment, and status-building, not on being content and happy. This is why I believe you have achieved at least one remarkable thing, but you don't remember it instantly or unintentionally undermine its importance.

I challenge you to make a list of your accomplishments. Sit down, pen and paper, and start brainstorming what you have accomplished. After 15 to 20 minutes of letting your brain flow down memory lane, you will start remembering bits and pieces of events, successes, and accomplishments you had forgotten entirely.

When I first did this exercise, I felt like a complete loser who was behind in life in every possible way. Then, I forced myself to sit down for 20 minutes and write my heart out. What came out wasn't as impressive as the CV of a world-class athlete, accomplished artist, or a seasoned CEO of a Fortune 500 company, but it was a decent start.

I started with the bare minimum, finishing high school, getting a driver's license, completing my degree after pausing once, and dropping out two times before that. I dived deeper for anything worth something. Finishing second at a swimming competition. Out-competing 50+ candidates for a junior position without experience after college. I managed to maintain strength training as a habit for three years, even if I skipped some days or weeks due to work.

The point of the list isn't to get you content with yourself. If you are reading this, you are hungry to be better and work on yourself. The accomplishment list is the anchor point you need to get momentum. It is the clear, tangible, and undeniable proof you are not a failure with no redeeming qualities and potential. Stick it to a wall right next to your desk, add it as wallpaper, or whatever allows you to look at it as much as possible. Let it remind you how much you've done already and how this is only the beginning.

Manage Negative Self-Talk With CBT

According to Stefan G. Hofmann and Anu Asnaani's meta-analysis study, CBT is one of the most widely studied therapeutic methods, with substantial evidence behind it after comparison with several other treatments and control conditions across multiple studies.[11]

CBT is not a universal solution to every mental health disorder, but it is specifically helpful for changing thought patterns and negative self-talk, because every CBT-based exercise centers around changing the way you think.

The core premise of traditional CBT states that your beliefs and convictions influence the thoughts passing through your mind every day and the automatic thoughts you have as a response to any event and experience. In turn, all those thoughts shape the experience you have of an event. They determine our feelings, physiological responses, and behavior as a consequence.

For example, imagine your significant other hasn't responded to your text messages in three hours. If you are in a securely attached relationship and feel confident in your worth as a person and a partner, you will think they are very busy and unavailable and shrug it off. However, if you have low self-worth, you are more likely to go down a negative spiral, feeling unloved, unworthy, and not deserving of attention while thinking of worrying reasons why they are not responding - they don't care enough, they prefer the company of someone else, etc.

The situation is the same in both scenarios, but how you view yourself and the beliefs you hold immensely changes your response. Traditional CBT seeks to get you from scenario two into scenario one by removing irrational thought patterns and beliefs that are not helpful, relevant to your circumstances, or based on reality. A common CBT exercise would include the following steps:

1. **Setup** - Choose a quiet environment where you won't be bothered by noise and distractions. Pick a pen and a piece of paper - a single piece, notebook, journal, etc. Ensure you have at least 20 to 30 minutes dedicated to this exercise.

2. **Awareness** - Change begins with awareness of what is bothering you. Begin writing everything that comes to mind, even if it seems unrelated, weird, and pointless. Eventually, you will see some worries, insecurities, and negative thoughts emerge.

3. **Narrow down** - You need to specify and pick a single thought pattern. Thinking of yourself as lazy, stupid, and not enough for others may feel similar because all those thoughts make you feel worthless and unhappy, but their root cause is usually different.

4. **Challenge the thought pattern** - Just writing down your thoughts is usually enough to create distance, making it easier to see them as subjective interpretations by your mind, which are not necessarily the objective truth. Once you do that, you can ask yourself. Is this thought true, and what evidence do I have for it? Is thinking this way helpful and aligned with my long-term goals?

5. **Reframe the internal narrative** - Rejecting thoughts altogether often doesn't work. It is much more helpful to find more meaningful interpretations that are aligned with your values and long-term goals. They carry a similar message and intention without the unnecessary hatred and harshness. For instance, saying, "It won't work and I won't succeed," can be replaced with, "I don't know if it will work or not, but at least I stand some chance if I try."

This exercise is not a miracle. Just like you'd need to work consistently for months before you see noticeable results, your brain has been wired to think in a specific way for months and even years. You need to consistently reflect on one set of negative thoughts and re-visit them a few times a week before your mind slowly begins to create new narratives.

Let's take an example of perfectionism. In theory, the belief and aspiration you need to be as perfect as possible doesn't sound harmful. However, once you reflect for a while, you realize perfectionism has its roots in low self-worth and feelings of inadequacy. You don't feel enough, so you need to overcompensate by being perfect. Very often, others critique and ridicule you, so being perfect will shield you from the disapproval, critique, and mockery of others.

Being perfect sounded like an excellent goal that you unconsciously began to believe over time. Only writing it all down on paper allowed you to get enough distance and see how you had followed this dogma of perfectionism without even questioning it once.

After challenging the thought pattern of perfectionism, you began to realize it wasn't very helpful to be a perfectionist. It created constant pressure and stress, which made you procrastinate even more. Most situations, tasks, and projects became high-stakes opportunities to prove your worth, which paralyzed you from action even further.

Now that you know the underlying reason behind your perfectionism - a desire to shield yourself from criticism and grow to be a more productive and successful person, it was easier to reframe your internal narrative into messages that were more helpful. For instance, saying to yourself how rejections, mistakes, and failures are necessary for growth and making success worth it helps you to cope with setbacks while giving you the momentum to keep going even if it didn't work out in the beginning.

Stop reading and try it out for yourself right now. Instead of reading further for 20 more minutes, you will find it much more helpful to incorporate what I have been saying until now by taking action.

Done?

When I asked clients and friends to do this exercise, the results fell into two categories.

The first found it helpful to stop, slow down, and reflect on the thoughts, which had previously felt like annoying and mentally exhausting background noise. It clarified what was wrong with their thinking and gave them a new direction to take, one less stressful and with a far more helpful mindset.

However, a second group of people found it helpful to reflect on what they were thinking but felt stuck in their beliefs despite the instructions. An invisible and unexplainable force stops them from changing their thought patterns, even if they are not helpful. I finally managed to crack this enigma after stumbling on the work of David Burns, one of Stanford's leading psychiatrists. He claims you can tear down the barrier by asking yourself a simple question as part of a thought experiment.

Overcoming Resistance To Change Negative Self-Talk

There is a red button in front of you with the label "negative self-talk killer." Once the button is pressed, all your negative thoughts will immediately disappear, now and forever.

Will you click the button?

Your immediate reaction is likely a loud "YES!". But think about it a bit. When I was first asked this question, I immediately thought of clicking the button, but the more I waited, the bigger my hesitation became. What kind of sane person would willingly choose to continue suffering with crippling thoughts they can't escape?

It sounds paradoxical, but there is a reason.

Most men would admit they don't like negative self-talk but find it necessary for personal growth. This is the harsh inner voice ringing with disappointment whenever you slack, the faint whisper constantly buzzing reminders of how little you are worth right now so you keep working hard, and the unimpressed critic who looks at every progress you make and says you can do better.

It is not a comforting, enjoyable, or peaceful experience, but you will grudgingly admit it often gets the job done. Some form of negative self-talk is not toxic. If your inner voice is complaining, then there must be a problem that needs to be solved. If you are unsatisfied with the results, you need to keep working harder to meet your approval. You will not be happy, but you can get more fit, learn new skills, and advance in your career.

Thinking of the bargain as a choice between personal and professional growth compared with immediate relief and happiness changes your final decision, right? Masculinity is often defined by persistence, commitment, and discipline despite suffering and struggle. To grow so you can be useful to others is seen by most men as a worthwhile sacrifice, even if it leads to some unhappiness. Finding some use in negative self-talk makes it so sticky and hard to change.

The problem with negative self-talk isn't its very existence but its intensity. Listening to music can help you stay alert and focused while working, but turning the volume to the maximum will take you out of the zone. Similarly, negative self-talk can be useful when done in moderation.

However, there are many circumstances where the volume and intensity of your negative self-talk become too much.

If you are accomplished and relatively successful, feeling crippled by insecurities and low self-esteem is not a worthwhile feeling. Your negative self-talk got you there but remained stuck to you despite not being as useful anymore. Similarly, while some presence of an inner critic can keep you accountable and motivated, too much can make you feel worthless and demoralized to the point where you give up trying altogether.

Knowing all of this now, what could be changed in our CBT exercise to make it worthwhile? We will retain the old five-step structure for setup, awareness, specialization, challenge, and reframing, but we will add one more step before reframing - acknowledging the usefulness of your negative self-talk.

Let's pick one common negative self-talk pattern: calling yourself stupid, incompetent, and other terms suggesting a lack of intelligence, abilities, and talent. We know insulting ourselves is not helpful, and it makes us feel miserable, but if you had to come up with reasons why such thoughts could potentially be useful, what would they be?

They show you have high standards for yourself. You are not content with being mediocre and just passing by. Instead, you aspire to be more and maximize your potential. Furthermore, when considered in the context of past failures, mistakes, and rejections, it shows you deeply care about your performance and usefulness to others, thus the emotional reaction when faced with challenges.

Go ahead and think of more reasons for a personally relevant example. It may sound absurd and counter-productive, but I encourage you to try it at least once.

We may have a subconscious desire to stay with negative beliefs because they are useful in paradoxical ways. This is David Burns' theory described in his best-seller "Feeling Good," and has also received scientific validation in studies by Mark E. Bouton[12].

According to him, your mind is not an irrational and crazy enemy seeking to make you feel useless and defeated. Every thought you have has a justification and reasoning behind it. Even if the end result is counter-productive, misguided, or no longer relevant, your beliefs and thoughts are formed with good intentions behind them - to protect you and help you flourish.

So far, we have become aware of our negative thoughts, narrowed them down into a single pattern bothering us at the moment, and begun to challenge this thought. Instead of trying to tear down what we usually think with aggression, our approach focuses on clearly weighing the pros and cons of our current mindset, attitude, and beliefs. Thinking of what is useful about our thoughts, instead of dismissing, devaluing, and hating on them, it becomes much easier to change because we are much less defensive.

When you get stuck in distorted patterns of negative thinking, it is very easy for your mind to think how you either believe in something or you don't. Especially for us with ADHD, the world and the way we think often boil down to an all-or-nothing approach. However, we will now take a different approach. Let's try to negotiate and lower the intensity of our negative self-talk instead of trying to destroy it altogether.

Thinking of the usefulness of your negative self-talk and seeking to decrease it instead of tearing it apart is essential to begin changing.

If your mind thinks you need to instantly change and transform massively, even if for the better, it is more likely to shut off and resist changing. For many people, reframing works as a final step only if their mind is sure it will reduce the intensity of what they are going for instead of eliminating it altogether.

For example, in a traditional CBT practice, you'd want to acknowledge how thoughts of being stupid and lazy were not helpful and hopefully reframe them into more meaningful interpretations, like "I am not as capable, experienced, and successful as I'd like to be right now, but I will keep trying until I get there."

With this enhanced approach, you will acknowledge how even those misguided and somewhat derogatory remarks had good intentions behind them. After weighing their potential usefulness, you will examine how strongly you believe and follow them right now. If it is a strong 8 out of 10 or even a 9, the point of the exercise would be to bring it down to 3 or 4 instead of trying to do a complete 180 by suddenly thinking you are a highly talented genius.

This compromise works on the same principle we discussed earlier when talking about the need for acceptance before you can even think of liking and loving yourself - slow and gradual change works best because your mind doesn't like huge and sudden changes to who you are.

Following this logic, you are much more likely to stick with a more accurate, kind, and empathetic interpretation of your circumstances if it's seen as a slight adjustment in the right direction instead of a complete change of course.

Chapter 3

Developing a Successful Career With ADHD

Today's chaotic economy is defined by a constantly rising inflation rate, unaffordable housing, and massive layoffs due to automation, AI, and outsourcing. In this environment, building a successful career to maintain a proper standard of living, material security, and freedom to enjoy life has never been more important.

This chapter will do a deep dive into how to have a positive connection with your career no matter what, offer a comprehensive set of strategies you can use to overcome any ADHD-related handicaps in the workplace and show how you can even take advantage of your different and unique brain to stand out and build a name for yourself.

The Complex Relationship Between a Man's Career and Self-Worth

It is very sad to observe how, globally, men are twice as likely to commit suicide compared to women. The death of a person from suicide is a tragedy no matter what, but that doesn't reduce the need to understand why there is such a stark difference.

Despite this need, little research has been done to explain the stark difference, but one Australian experiment offers some clues. The researchers reviewed the language used in the suicide letters of men who had attempted to take their lives. After more than a hundred entries were reviewed, they noticed the same words over and over again - useless, worthless, waste, burden, etc.[13]

This makes a lot of sense because masculinity is often defined by a man's ability to be useful to his family, community, and society as a whole. For decades, centuries, and even millennia, being a man meant being the breadmaker, provider, and the primary source of material stability in the family. We used to feel a sense of purpose by providing financial security to our loved ones by working.

However, times are fundamentally changing with the emancipation of women and their massive enrolment in the workplace, the decline in marriage rates and the typical family structure, and the modernization of dating norms.

On the one hand, this is liberating for men who feel suffocated by society's expectations. Those who didn't want to be defined by their career alone and didn't enjoy the idea of overworking themselves to death without an opportunity to spend much time with their partner and family. On the other hand, the lack of certainty and a clear path to meaning has left many young men to plunge into existential crises where they feel lost, not knowing the right path.

It's true that your career does not have to define your self-worth. There are factors outside of your control that can significantly influence the trajectory of your career.

People get laid off on a massive scale because a company is not profitable enough. You could get fired for the mistake of upper management. It's likely that at some point, you will not receive a promotion you rightfully deserve because of nepotism. Even when highly competent, you may enter an oversaturated market in an economic downturn, meaning there will be no jobs. Unfortunately, no matter what you do, you may face some form of discrimination based on your background, ethnicity, and character.

So, what are you supposed to do if your career is not thriving or you want to focus on other parts of your life but feel pressured to conform? Finding yourself respectable no matter what you have done in life and acknowledging your talent, potential, and competence sounds good on paper. But how do you turn feel-good self-talk into reality?

Your beliefs are often based on and justified with evidence, so when you want to improve your self-esteem, you have to turn your attention toward the other areas in your life where you have grown and created value for yourself and others. The proof you need is likely already there, but you have overlooked it.

There are a lot of things in life that we take as a given, like consistently working out five times a week for years, being in a long-term relationship with a loving partner, and still keeping the spark going, hobbies that you have stuck with and developed over the areas. Even simple but deep conversations late at night with a friend where you shared your struggles and offered advice when they were at their lowest are amazing feats.

We often get so caught up in wanting to be more and not feeling enough that we forget how much we have achieved because it's not specific or quantifiable. Workforces you to think in terms of goals, milestones, KPIs, and tangible growth, but you can't quantify the laughter of your child when spending time with them, the sense of camaraderie, the hard work you did pulling yourself out of the rut every single time, and other key achievements. Just because they are not as visible doesn't mean they are not there.

By seeing how you have progressed, improved, and created value in the world, even outside of your career, you can build a genuine sense of self-worth. But what if, despite looking, you still feel as though that's enough? The harsh truth is that sometimes, no matter how much you reflect and look at the trajectory of your life, self-talk can not remove the sense that you are behind. Very often, you can't just erase a lack of confidence.

However, just because you don't feel good enough right now doesn't mean you have to be in this state forever. In the very worst case, where you feel at rock bottom, fallen behind, and struggling to get up, you can still retain some confidence. Not because the past and present are going well but because you can work on making your future better. But to get this momentum, you need to focus on the next step ahead, not on the finish line.

If you want to lose 50 pounds, every 5 pounds is a major victory, and you shouldn't celebrate only if you nail the goal perfectly. If you want to improve your career prospects, just getting a call back for a test interview with a Fortune 500 company is an improvement, even if you don't get the job.

Behind every life-changing transformation, there are hundreds of small victories. Confidence can not be built in an instant; it is a statue composed of a thousand pieces, and you can slowly pick up and place one of them for every small achievement you make on the way.

The ADHD Struggle With Careers

Have you ever dropped out of university, switched degrees halfway through, or miraculously finished your degree only to start working in a completely different field? When it comes to your career, how many jobs or fields have you tried before settling down, or perhaps you are still searching for the ideal job and work environment?

Finding the right career with ADHD can feel like searching for a needle in a haystack. Most corporate 9-to-5 jobs are mundane, repetitive, and highly structured - the total opposite of what your brain needs to remain stimulated and engaged. Even if you successfully begin to settle down in a field, the impulsive urge whispering, "What if we try this instead?" never fully stops ringing in your mind. The ADHD brain craves novelty, variety, and enjoyment, which often fundamentally clashes with conventional careers.

The ADHD struggle doesn't end with choosing and sticking to a career. You've likely noticed how your different brain creates all sorts of obstacles in the workplace. In situations where you are:

- Rushing to be on time because of the chaos at home and your lack of time awareness always gets you late and potentially in trouble.
- Feeling overwhelmed with the endless amounts of tasks you must cover and struggling to prioritize which matters the most.
- Procrastinating with emails and administrative work, knowing you will do the real work only when your body injects you with an insane amount of cortisol and adrenaline at the last moment.
- Managing to hyper-focus at long last, only to be interrupted by another pointless meeting.
- Fidgeting under the table with your feet and struggling not to zone out.
- Feeling stupid to ask a second time for the details of the upcoming project because they said so much, and you can't keep track.
- Knowing you need a written summary and notes to work optimally but conforming to the culture of verbal communication because you feel too awkward to ask otherwise.

The fear of failure, making careless mistakes, rejection for initiatives and promotions, and falling behind compared to your co-workers are all very real. If, despite all of those setbacks and additional challenges, you still have a job that pays the bills, then this is a cause for celebration.

Not all people with ADHD are so fortunate. According to a national US study, only half of between 8 and 9 million adults with

ADHD can hold a full-time job. Even if they remain employed, their wages are comparatively lower than those of their peers. The average boss is risk-averse. They'd prefer not to hire a person with a registered disability, and if they are already overworked and stressed, making an effort for special accommodation doesn't seem worth it17.

ADHD creates numerous disadvantages at work, and I am sure you know it. I'm not saying this to get you depressed and sink your hopes. Rather, it's only through an objective look at reality and all its challenges that we can most effectively run to navigate the obstacles in our way.

Picking The Right Career – Finding ADHD-Friendly Options

One of the most heated and ongoing debates in career guidance is between people who say, "Follow your dreams and do what you love," and those who counter with, "Careers are about earning money. Following your dreams will make you end up poor."

At first thought, the latter appears more appealing. Careers should be about hard work, discipline, and sacrificing time, effort, sweat, tears, and blood to make a name for yourself and succeed. Nothing could sound more masculine than the mental strength and resilience of a person doing what needs to be done, even if they don't like what they are doing at all, right?

No, this couldn't be further from the truth.

I get what you are thinking. It is not wise to completely follow your dreams. Going all in on a niche hobby, trying to become a national rockstar with your college band, or becoming a social media influencer or video game streamer is not going to work for most people.

However, neither will grinding yourself to death while believing in a version of success and career building that romanticizes suffering, misery, and mental exhaustion. Just liking the future version of you who will be successful in the future and the wealth you will have is not enough if you have ADHD.

We've already established how having ADHD means you are very likely to be chronically under-stimulated and more sensitive to boredom. This means it is much harder to continuously do what you don't enjoy doing. Maybe you can pull it off for weeks or months for a project or two, but you shouldn't base your whole career on getting long-term gratification. The ADHD brain is very much blind to ambiguous future rewards and needs stimulation right now.

You don't have to be absolutely in love with your job and every single aspect of it, but when choosing a career and getting the appropriate certifications and experience, there are a few rules to make the ADHD-friendly choice. Those include:

- Jobs where you can complete smaller tasks or where you can easily break down tasks to make it easier to start and get quickly rewarded for working
- Jobs with clearly defined and upcoming deadlines close in the future, like a few days or a week from now, so you can feel a sense of urgency

- Jobs giving you intrinsic motivation to do them because of the meaningful impact you have on others, or the enjoyment you get from the day-to-day process
- Jobs with dynamic schedules where most days don't feel the same, and you have lots of variety and novelty in your environment
- Jobs where you can have more independence, self-initiative and room to create your own systems, routines, and to lead relevant to your projects and creative initiatives

If you were to ask people with ADHD about what they do for a living, the most common jobs you'd see are - graphic designers, writers, journalists, firefighters, critical care nurses and ER doctors, teachers, chefs, entrepreneurs, and professionals with lots of outdoor work. The vast majority of those examples fulfill the criteria we've set above. I am sure you also have additional personal likings and preferences, so write them down and make a list of what makes you feel engaged at work.

It's not that you can't survive a job and working environment that isn't ADHD-friendly. I'm sure you can pull through anything. Rather, it's not worth doing if you have the option because of the price you have to pay. Working twice as hard as everyone else to stay concentrated and avoid mistakes in an excruciatingly boring job is exhausting for a day and soul-crushing if done for months or years.

Staying Productive At Work No Matter What

You can get more productive at work by creating individual systems personalized to your workplace or by asking for accommodation and communicating with the higher-ups for assistance.

What kind of a productivity system you should develop is based on the type of work you are doing. A corporate 9-to-5 will look very different from a 12-hour shift at a warehouse.

However, creating as much clarity about the work process, list of tasks, deadlines, and any other relevant details is always an excellent idea. This is because written guides and instructions won't always be there. They may be outdated and not in-depth enough to capture all the nuances of the workplace, and some employers are not very cooperative in giving you additional instructions, even if it's in their best interest.

The easiest way to intentionally create clarity is with a note-taking system. Over time, if you work in the same place, you will get a strong intuition of what needs to be done and where, but the note-taking system can speed up the process significantly while making you feel less overwhelmed and anxious about whether you are missing something or not.

The premise is very simple - working memory issues may make you forget important things, so take note of absolutely everything. You can sort out what's truly worth expanding on or discarding entirely later, but whenever anyone mentions anything, you listen and re-phrase it in your own words somewhere. It could be a digital note-taking app or a little pocket notebook you carry around. Whatever is comfortable to you. The point is to delegate memorization to take notes so your brain is entirely focused on thinking.

If somebody mentions an upcoming deadline, write it down. If you have a random thought related to a project, write it down. If you are discussing upcoming initiatives in a meeting and the details are mostly mentioned with verbal communication, write it down. Even if people say you will remember and there's no need to write it down, you know what to do. In the beginning, it may be a bit tedious, but after you've done it for a while, it will become entirely automatic.

This is a universally beneficial system, but you can create your own based on the issues you are facing in your workplace. For instance, if you get overwhelmed by the disorganization around your desk, then you can make it a rule to organize anything back into place if it takes less than 5 minutes. If you feel paralyzed by the countless tasks on your to-do list, you can try organizing based on upcoming deadlines, so urgency will dictate which one is a priority.

Even with intentional effort, staying productive at work can sometimes be an issue because of the environment around you. This is especially true for noise and other distractions, which can get you off course.

It becomes much easier to concentrate if you have a strict separation of work-related devices and personal belongings. Impulses to give into temptations are automatic, so they work on associations. If you put your phone and home laptop away and don't browse or game on the company's devices, paying attention is easier due to the separation of environments.

Speaking to your high-ups and asking for accommodation can be an excellent idea, but it entirely depends on the work culture and the personalities of the people in charge. For instance, working with noise-canceling headphones shouldn't be an issue, but whether you can get special treatment by moving to work in a quieter area will depend on company resources and your boss' attitude. You don't have to explicitly say you have ADHD, especially if you fear stigma. Instead, you can say you are much more productive in quiet environments based on past experience.

Unfortunately, even if you have the perfect environment, a ready-to-do list, and a clear vision, instructions, and information on what needs to be done, you may still struggle to get started or work in general. This is not an issue if you work in the service sector where something happens every moment, and you have no choice but to do work. However, it can be a huge problem if you work remotely or in a corporate setting with big projects where the deadline is far into the future.

How to Create a Sense of Urgency and Intrinsic Motivation Anytime You Need

You can overcome this action paralysis by doing something you love or trying to create a sense of urgency and fulfillment. The first option is much harder to do but highly successful if you pull it off. If you are working on something with freedom and room for creativity and genuine expression, then trying to stop and take a break will likely be much harder than starting.

However, the vast majority of people don't have this luxury, so we have to get creative and intentionally create a sense of urgency and intrinsic motivation, even if there isn't one in the present. Here are the strategies that have worked for me and the people I've coached:

Start Ridiculously Small With Everything

Even if you dread cleaning, you must have had moments where cleaning a few dishes turned into an all-day re-organization and cleaning of everything. Very often, you can get into a task or project flow once you start and warm up for a bit. Since resistance is highest at the start, you can motivate yourself by making the entry action ridiculously small, so it feels absurd not to do so.

Make It Competitive

Manually stacking boxes in the warehouse, writing emails, or doing paperwork feels mundane due to how repetitive it is. Back in the day, my only salvation was making it competitive. It was either through an explicit bet with a buddy at work or by secretly observing my peers and picking high performers I wanted to beat. It didn't cost me anything, and very often, the notion of competing directly with them instantly clicked a button in me.

Gamification

You've heard of the app Duolingo, right? It's everywhere. Unlike many other useful language software programs,

Duolingo works because it is very gamified. You have daily challenges, quests, level-ups, etc. With ADHD, finding happiness at the finish line is not enough if it feels like it will take you forever to finish. This is why you can gamify tasks at work and business projects using apps like TaskHero, Habitica, LifeUp, and others. If you enjoy video games, you can almost turn your life into one.

The Pomodoro Technique

The premise of the Pomodoro technique is very simple - you work for 25 to 40 minutes and rest for 5 to 20 minutes, depending on your preference. Many see it as beneficial because you organize your work in time slots and balance work with rest. However, the bigger benefit for people with ADHD is how it creates a sense of urgency due to the short time interval you have. Furthermore, if your work gets interrupted halfway through, it feels much easier to pick right up.

Find an Accountable Buddy

Sometimes, just working next to someone else is enough to get you started since it creates pressure to perform. If you are working from home, there are Discord servers dedicated to studying and working with others on video chat, or you can just go to a cafe surrounded by strangers.

Not enough? You can increase the stakes by promising to check up for 5-10 minutes at the end of the day to see how much you did. If that's also not enough, you can raise the stakes further by promising to send your buddy money if you don't get a set amount of work done. I was initially reluctant to commit but quickly fell in line after losing more than a hundred dollars!

Gear Up To Bypass Time Blindness

Time blindness is one of the biggest culprits for being late to work and spending a whole day not working if your job is remote. If your internal clock is faulty, you must design an environment that will compensate.

Get yourself multiple clocks - one on the wrist, one in the shower, and one for each room. Old-fashioned clocks are better than checking your telephone because each click can turn into a social media binge. Furthermore, leave yourself reminders. Either digitally write everything down in a calendar that will automatically ring an alarm or use physical reminders, like sticky notes, whiteboards, and even writing down something quickly in the mirror so you don't forget.

Clean Your Home to Clear Your Mind

One of the most neglected distractions is having a cluttered and messy home, making it virtually impossible to stay productive while working from home. In my early 20s, my one-room apartment was filled with dirty piles of clothes, chairs with junk, and dirty dishes. The instant I was back home, I became miserable and demotivated.

If you are busy and not a cleaning freak, the easiest way to get your home in order is to go the minimalist route. The less you own, the less you have to deal with. During the weekend, dedicate a whole day to getting everything in order. If you are not actively using something, throw it away, and from this point onward, have an alarm that automatically goes off in the evening, forcing you to clean for the day for at least 15 minutes so it doesn't accumulate again.

I understand that you do not have your dream career yet and need immediate relief and a productivity boost, so I've offered all those strategies. However, doing something you love feels like swimming along a river current instead of desperately fighting against the force pulling you in the other direction.

This is why it's essential to manage your motivation but simultaneously work on finding employment opportunities, freelancing projects, business gigs, or anything else that will not only give you material security but also resonate with your needs for engagement, stimulation, enjoyment, and meaning.

Taking Advantage of Hyper Focus – How To Enter a Flow State for Focus and Motivation

When you do something you enjoy, you are engaged and stimulated. Your brain is firing up, producing neurotransmitters like dopamine and norepinephrine. It is easier to focus than to pay attention elsewhere while doing something you dislike or loathe, which creates the opposite effect - keeping your attention in one place feels like an uphill battle.

Ideally, you want to be doing something that gets you to hyper-focus and enter a flow state. This is a state of consciousness where you are not thinking, reflecting, or ruminating much, if at all. You are single-handedly focused and fully captivated by a task, so much so that you can do a day's work in two or three hours. Some activities, like skateboarding, surfing, football, and video games, have often been described as optimal for flow building.[14]

Unfortunately, most of us can not easily make a career out of many obvious flow-building activities. Still, we can follow certain steps to increase the chance of getting into a flow state.

First, you have to know about the preconditions for flow that lead to intrinsic motivation - a desire to do the activity without considering external reward or punishment. Those are curiosity, passion, mastery, purpose, and autonomy. Any of them lacking can reduce how motivated you feel.

For instance, you may have felt many fluctuations during college or high school because you were curious and passionate about the material, but academic rules and limitations constrained you. Once you graduate and get a job with lots of autonomy to operate as you wish, your motivation and sense of purpose may have skyrocketed, helping you feel more motivated constantly.

Second, you need to find the sweet spot between boredom and anxiety. If an activity is too boring, you won't be motivated. What would be the point of trying if you already know it and there is nothing to gain?

Similarly, if an activity is too challenging to a point where it creates crippling anxiety about your performance, then you will freeze, shut down, or run away from the task altogether. The sweet spot is a task slightly above your level that is stressful enough to get you going.

How to Create and Maintain A Flow State

Here is what you can immediately implement to increase the chance of staying in a flow state for as long as possible.

Create Associations in Your Environment

Environments wire us toward certain activities. Think of your bed and how you get lazy and sleepy whenever you lay down, making you unable to study it effectively. First, dedicate a location exclusively toward one activity so your brain associates it with only that type of work.

Second, experiment to see which environment works best for you. For some people, being very minimalistic, with minimal sounds and noises, and only the laptop in front of them works best. Others prefer working in the presence of other people and listening to classical music and white, brown, and pink noise playlists on YouTube to stay in the zone.

Remove Distractions From Your Working Space

You can reduce the time you stay distracted from 30 to 5 minutes if you put your phone on the top shelf in another room instead of right in front of you.

Turn on focus mode when working, install apps and plugins to block out all distracting sites, and create barriers to anything that could completely immerse your attention, like your phone, e-reader, other devices, etc. It is much easier to come back to work after getting stressed and pacing the room for 2 minutes instead of when you get sucked into social media or an internet rabbit hole.

Survive the warm-up

Entering a flow state does not happen instantly, like a snap of your fingers. It is a gradual, difficult process initially but gets much easier after 15 to 20 minutes.

I start ridiculously small. If I have a project with multiple steps, I write them all down in almost absurd detail - open the laptop, create a title, write the first two sentences, write two more sentences, etc.

This way, ambiguity and the sense of being overwhelmed are minimal. Doing something feels almost frictionless because you need to do more. But that's fine because getting familiar and comfortable with the task is the point. Just like you warm up in the gym so your muscles are ready, you want to warm up your mind for 15-20 minutes before the engagement begins.

Creating Urgency When You Have None

Some people get overwhelmed while trying to start and give up, but others can't even take the very first step. This is action paralysis caused by executive dysfunction - you know you have to work, but you can't start no matter what. You can overcome this mental block by creating a sense of urgency. Set up an alarm for 30 minutes and let it run down. The more time passes, the more you will feel an urge to do something, at least before the time starts.

Normalize Short Breaks

Do you ever get jittery, restless, and anxious while hyper-focused on a task? It's like your system's overheating. One moment, you are typing out hundreds of words, and the next, you slow down and keep bouncing your leg back and forth.

Sorry to break it to you, but the ADHD brain is not like those YouTube compilations of workaholics who record themselves studying and working for 14 hours straight. Distractions and snapping out of your work trance happen when this unpleasant feeling gets too much. You can prevent it by simply stopping for a few minutes to recharge.

Preventing Your Breaks From Turning Into Stops

When working with ADHD, you win not by working for 12 hours straight but by returning your attention back to the task after stopping for a short while. When we think of breaks, we think of browsing social media, playing a video game, watching a show, etc. This is not a break but a rest. You rest by doing something you enjoy and having fun.

Breaks are supposed to recharge you and prepare you for the next round of work. Your stimulation-craving brain has no reason to return to the boring work with little immediate reward if you have just spent 25 minutes browsing Reddit or TikTok. Set the alarm for 5 to 15 minutes maximum, lay down staring at the wall, pace around, do nothing, and just exist.

Hacking Your Motivation With Parkinson's Law

Work expands to fill the time you have given yourself to finish a task. Paradoxically, I used to be much more productive when I had only an hour and a half to work on my side business during the weekday than the whole day during the weekend. There was no urgency, meaning my mind could infinitely rationalize starting later.

You can do the same intentionally by limiting how much you can work in a given day. After three hours, you must immediately stop. You will feel like you are missing out, but this pain will motivate you to do more in tomorrow's time window.

Hyper-focus and getting in a flow state can lead to an immense amount of productivity, but it requires intention. You may have negative associations with hyper-focus because you think of it as another negative part of ADHD, the one that makes you spend 11 hours on social media glued to the scream, or the reason behind one curious click on an article leading you to jump into a huge internet rabbit hole with dozens more articles and Wikipedia pages.

Hyper-focusing on pointless things is bound to happen if you have no vision and clearly defined goals in life. In this very moment, can you say out loud what overarching purpose your actions are centering around? Most of you have a general idea. Personally, I want to help as many people as possible by teaching them to work with their unique brains and how to overcome common cognitive biases when trying to be productive.

However, just the vision of what you want to do and who you want to be is not enough. Entering a meaningful and productive flow state requires clear goals that leave no uncertainty about what you must do. My vision of helping others can be narrowed to writing this book for all of you, and more specifically, writing 1000 words a day and, even more specifically, writing this very heading before I think of anything else.

Take what you want to do and specify it similarly. Ideally, the endpoint should be a small goal you can achieve in 30 minutes or less. It will always be easier to get lost in social media, video games, and other kinds of distractions and addictions because they offer immediate pleasure and relief from discomfort while goals seem to take forever to pay off.

But you can change all that once you have a crystal clear vision and very specific goals because if it takes less than 30 minutes to make progress, then you are bound to get a dopamine spike after the alarm goes off. It is all about momentum.

Chapter 4

Lifestyle Habits and Routines To Improve ADHD Symptoms

Preventing the worst problems that arise from executive dysfunction and ADHD, in general, is a preferable strategy to figuring out how to act in the moment after a mistake has already happened. For instance, working on reducing impulsivity and increasing self-control prevents spontaneous purchases instead of leaving you to worry about how you will pay rent after going above your budget.

In many cases, the debate around our ability to treat ADHD with lifestyle changes turns into black-and-white arguments and straw-manning. One side goes against the scientific literature and claims enough outdoor activities, proper dieting, and supplements will cure your condition, while the other side hides behind the label of permanence and claims it is pointless to try and make your ADHD better.

As always, the sweet spot is in the middle.

ADHD is a neurodevelopmental disorder leading to permanent and irreversible changes in the brain, but having a different brain doesn't doom you forever. As a person with ADHD, you are more likely to experience specific symptoms, but how frequently you feel them and how intense, painful, and disturbing they are depends on multiple factors.

This chapter will go through the essential lifestyle habits, routines, and activities you should focus on including in your life to reduce the severity of your ADHD symptoms. We will discuss both why they are so important and how you can integrate them into your everyday life with step-by-step protocols.

Create An Active Lifestyle and Embrace Regular Exercise

Regular aerobic exercise and strength training are often associated with a more fit and toned body. However, by training your body, you are also sharpening your mind. Since ADHD is a condition connected with a disruption in neurotransmitter activity, exercising can be immensely helpful because it is a natural way for your body to release endorphins, norepinephrine, dopamine, and other healthy brain chemicals.[15]

If you've ever felt the runner's high after running a few miles, felt in sync with your body and slowed down significantly while doing yoga, or felt relief from how silent your mind was after an intense gym session, now you know why.

The dopamine and norepinephrine improve alertness, concentration, and motivation, while the endorphins released after a workout make you more resilient to stress and lift your mood. According to the current scientific literature, regular exercise is one of the most reliable and beneficial ways to feel less stimulation-deprived and to reduce anxiety, hyperactivity, and feelings of being overwhelmed.

You probably already knew exercise made you more healthy, but now you know it can alleviate ADHD symptoms. All that remains is for you to make it part of your everyday life, which is easier said than done for many.

Strategies to Make Exercise Easier

Here are some of the strategies that have worked for me and the people I've worked with:

Begin With Something You Enjoy Doing

The more you dread the workout, the more resistance you will feel, which would be enough to find excuses and skip the session if you already feel exhausted and low on motivation. If it feels like a burden, then it's likely not sustainable.

For instance, if you find it depressing to work from home, go to a public gym. If you dread running, sprinting, or swimming and don't want to go out, try jump rope, burpees, and kettlebell swinging at home. There are endless options. You just need to start with one. What you enjoy is what you will consistently do over the long term, so it's best to stick with that.

Try To Have Some Form of Activity Almost Every day

Depending on your schedule and how busy and exhausted you are on a particular day, you won't always be available to dedicate yourself to a workout fully. The goal should be to pull yourself up even when feeling down. It doesn't have to be hard or even challenging. A 15-minute walk outside, three sets of push-ups, 10 minutes on the bike at home, or any other small effort is enough. This way, you strengthen the habit and teach yourself not to be a perfectionist.

Be Flexible Without Fear

Many people find it most convenient for routines and habits to be strictly placed in their schedule. For instance, you either work out at 6:30 am or miss your opportunity.

Although this creates a sense of consistency, structure, and automatic urgency when the time comes, such routines often collapse due to the uncertainty in life. If you wake up late, have an emergency in the morning, or go out of town to visit your parents without access to the gym, the routine is gone. This is why you have to allow yourself to be flexible. Even if not perfect, a different workout is better than no activity.

Create Rituals

Your brain works on associations. You wake up, and it's time to wash your teeth and face and shower. You see your phone, and you instantly think of browsing Reddit, Instagram, TikTok, or YouTube. By doing the same activity before each workout, you prime your brain to anticipate and automatically start the workout after you are done with your ritual.

Personally, I pace around and listen to some motivational speakers, like David Goggins, on a YouTube playlist before doing strength training. The more it gets you motivated and hyped up, the better.

Don't Forget To Warm Up After Long Breaks

Everyone tells you to do warm-up sets and stretches no matter what you do to avoid the risk of injury and improve performance.

Similarly, if you are sick, taking care of family, on vacation, and life has generally gotten in the way, you also need to warm up your brain to exercise. If you've fallen off the routine of doing 20 sets with dumbbells and weights four times a week, you can't come back and bust another 20 in the beginning. You need to reduce the volume, do far less for the first one or two workouts, and gradually build up to your previous peak.

Don't Be Afraid of Dopamine Stacking When Working Out

If you've seen neuroscientists on YouTube, like Andrew Huberman, or motivational male speakers, they always say you shouldn't be listening to music or doing anything else while working out. Either because it's not healthy or not masculine.

This is not good advice for a person with ADHD. If you feel like crap but still want to work out, very often, the exercises themselves will not be stimulating enough, or the hormone and brain chemicals released will happen after, but you need it now. Do whatever you need to do to get through a workout without shame. Personally, I watch a show while doing my cardio because I find it boring otherwise.

Turn It Into Part of Your Identity

If you see yourself as a runner, you have no choice but to do your miles three times a week. However, if you see running as optional and something that'd be beneficial to do if you had the will and motivation, then you are much more likely to skip sessions or drop the effort altogether. If your identity is strongly connected to the sport and type of training you do, you are more likely to preserve this identity, making it easier to stay consistent and progress.

For instance, I have a dedicated room for working out, with posters of bodybuilders. When I allow myself to watch YouTube or social media, I focus solely on gym-related content, so a larger part of my time is spent on anything related to my aspiring identity.

Get an Accountability Buddy When Working Out

Sometimes, no matter what, you will not want to get out of bed, and the only way to do a workout is to be dragged out by someone else.

Having a gym buddy, sports partner, or an accountability person in any setting not only gets you motivated, hyped up, and competitive during each training session, but it guarantees you will show up because you don't want to let them down. Similarly to the strategy of identity building, you leave yourself no choice. Working out is inevitable, not an option, because you need to show up for them.

The benefits of exercise don't end with an improved mood, less anxiety and overwhelming thoughts, and higher alertness and focus.

Outside of the direct biological positives, the very act of consistently exercising can greatly improve your self-confidence. Your self-esteem is bound to rise when you have a long-term commitment, make slow but steady progress, and very visibly see how you are getting better because you pack muscle, lose weight, break performance plateaus, learn new exercises, get compliments from people, and win competitions if you compete in any sports.

Enhance Your Sleep Hygiene

People with ADHD tend to struggle to fall asleep at night, feel restless throughout the night and wake up before the intended time, have difficulty waking up in the morning, and feel tired and unrested throughout the day.

The clearest connection between ADHD and troubles with sleep has to do with the effect your symptoms have on your mental health. If you constantly feel overwhelmed, rushing to do something, and your brain has a dozen thoughts and desires swirling in your mind, it's not easy to calm your mind and fall asleep.[16]

Personally, I've noticed that my hyperactivity can get even worse if I wasn't very physically active during the day. Maybe it was because I had tons of pent-up energy that didn't receive an outlet.

Some limited research has shown ADHD correlates with sleeping disorders, like circadian rhythm disorders.

This is a disruption in the biological clock that synchronizes all your behavioral and physical changes throughout the day and makes you fall asleep and wake up at a certain time. Anecdotally, many people with ADHD describe themselves as night owls, preferring to go to sleep between 2 and 3 am and waking up at 10 to 11 am instead of the typical 12 am to 8 am sleep cycle.

Unfortunately, in our culture, sleep has long been seen as a commodity to be sacrificed for future gain. I'm sure you've seen posts, videos, and speeches of famous people claiming to work 14-16 hours to achieve success, waking up at 5 or 6 am to have more time to work, claiming even an hour spent sleeping and resting could be to work, grind, and hustle. The basis for those claims comes from the outdated belief it is fine to sacrifice some rest and quality sleep so you can be better off in the future.

This couldn't be further from the truth.

First, the downsides of sleep deprivation can be immediately felt even with less than 6 hours of sleep for a single night, and they don't completely recover even if you nap during the day. What's especially worrying is that many of the negative side effects of sleep deprivation are very similar to ADHD symptoms - forgetfulness, lack of alertness and focus, mood swings, lack of motivation, binge eating, etc. This means being sleep-deprived with ADHD only magnifies your symptoms even more, making it virtually impossible to be highly productive.[17]

Secondly, the premise of "work now, rest later" rests on the assumption that sacrificing sleep is worth it because every hour spent on work is the same - the 15th and 16th hour you spent at midnight is equally productive to your first hours in the morning.

We both know this simply isn't true.

I'm sure you've realized for yourself, through trial and error, that you have a few productive hours in you most days, and everything above that requires much more effort to pull out something. This is the law of diminishing returns - the more you do something, the less you get out of each individual unit, or in this case, time block.

In summary, sleep is not only the foundation for you to feel well, be productive, and have a stable mood, but it is the essential rest through which you reduce the risk for every single serious condition, like obesity, diabetes, cardiovascular disease, depression, and others. If you skip 3 hours of sleep at night, that's nearly 1000 a year. I highly doubt that 1000 extra hours a year in a groggy and zombified state are worth the risk and the certain reduction in your total productivity.

I know how, at the moment, when you feel overwhelmed with tasks and hard-pressed to not miss deadlines at work, not fall behind, and keep up your great performance at work, it can feel like a worthwhile sacrifice because you gain time. However, this is just an illusion. In 95% of cases, it is better to try to sleep and get at least 6 hours, if not seven and a half minimum, instead of trying to work while your eyes are closing or saturating yourself with ungodly amounts of caffeine.

If you are a person who's sleeping less than six hours a night, I have hopefully convinced you to make a change. You may not trust me enough to permanently change your entire routine and way of life, and I'd understand. However, you owe it to yourself to at least test out an alternative way of living. Try to sleep at least seven and a half hours every night for six weeks. If it works, that's great, your life is better. If not, at least you will have no doubts about your way of life and feel good you proved me wrong.

I don't mean to appear judgemental and accusatory. I've had days, weeks, and even whole months where I was sleep-deprived.

My advice comes after deep regret and remorse for the way I treated my body and mind in the past and after reflecting on how much more I could have done had I not gambled with my sleep the way I did. I get why sleep is not a priority for many of you, even if you know it's important - you are swamped with so much else, and sleep naturally happens one way or another, so you passively go to sleep and wake up without putting much thought into it.

You can acknowledge how you didn't take it seriously in the past without allowing this mistake to keep burdening you into the future. Take responsibility now and put intention into your sleep hygiene because sleeping better is not a sacrifice and trade-off with something else you could have done instead. Rather, it is the precondition and foundation upon which you can have alertness, focus, critical thinking, creativity, energy, and motivation.

Enough theory. Let's get started with the practical part. Here is a science-based step-by-step protocol on how to improve the quality of your sleep:

Make It Into a Routine

Your circadian rhythm gives a very significant but often neglected hint about what your body wants - routine. You are most efficient when you consistently go to sleep at the same time and wake up roughly at the same time.

Trying to go to sleep and wake up at approximately the same time every day can improve the quality of your sleep. Furthermore, it makes it easier to fall asleep and feel rested, freeing up at least an hour during the day.

Reduce Your Exposure to Blue Light in the Evening

Your body can't distinguish between light from your TV, phone, or laptop and the light from the sun. Your circadian rhythm signals your body to fall asleep when blue light exposure is significantly reduced, so by taking a break from sources of such light 1-2 hours before bed, you can fall asleep faster. You choose how extreme to be.

Personally, I only have a small lamp in one corner and read on my e-reader. Some people I know use blue-light-blocking glasses and do yoga in complete darkness for 30 minutes before sleep.

Relax Before Going To Sleep

Being stressed signals your body to be alert and wary of some danger threatening you, even if there is no real danger.

Unless you have a very immediate deadline for tomorrow on an unfinished task, project, or assignment, working two or fewer hours before sleep is highly counterproductive. You will not get much done and mess up your sleep because you will feel anxious and restless in bed, still thinking about the work. Two more hours at night don't justify risking an entire day's productivity tomorrow.

Lower Your Body Temperature

Your circadian rhythm is not only influenced by daylight but also by the temperature around you. The colder it is, preferably enough to reduce your core temperature by 2-3 degrees Fahrenheit or 1 degree Celsius, the easier it is to fall asleep.

Nobody can deny that wrapping in a warm blanket during the winter is much more comfortable than sleeping almost naked during the summer. This is because colder temperatures make your body more receptive to falling asleep. Opening the window, taking a warm shower before bed, or avoiding a lot of movement and especially highly intensive workouts are all great ways to keep your body temperature low and prepare for better sleep.

Check Your Diet During the Later Part of the Day

Many people with ADHD are highly sensitive to caffeine. They get a buzz and drink multiple cups a day like it is water because the beverage acts as a stimulant, keeping them alert for a short while. It is essential for self-medication.

Unfortunately, it can wreak havoc on your sleep, so avoid anything containing caffeine 10 to 12 hours before you sleep. Furthermore, you want to have your last meals around 6 to 8 hours before you sleep and stop snacking during the night so your body is not kept awake due to the need to metabolize all the food you are eating.

Light Exposure

Earlier, we mentioned issues with circadian rhythm coordination. The only way to alleviate symptoms of a disorder in your biological clock is to give it stronger cues so it can become more accurate and fall in sync.

The easiest way to do this is to have direct exposure to light for at least 5 to 10 minutes in the morning. Walk the dog, go shopping in the morning, throw out the trash, go for a walk around the home, etc. If you don't want to go out, there are powerful lights designed specifically for circadian therapy you can buy online to create a similar effect.

Supplements as a Last-Measure Resort

The world of supplements is a gigantic rabbit hole full of contradictory science and contrasting personal anecdotes. Some of the most popular natural supplements are L-theanine, magnesium bisglycinate, zinc, valerian, and glycine.

If you take any medications, speak with a medical professional. Melatonin is the most popular and effective based on research, but you should get a consultation with a doctor first because you need it in the right dosage and for a set period. It is a temporary solution to get you on the right track, not a replacement for a lack of proper sleep hygiene.

Taking Steps Towards a More Healthy Diet

After a restful sleep and being active during the day, having a balanced and healthy diet is the last cornerstone of fundamental habits and activities you ought to intentionally maintain and improve. Since ADHD leads to impairments in brain function and disruptions in brain chemistry, giving your body the fuel it needs to create enough neurotransmitters and properly feed your brain circuits is essential to reduce the severity and frequency of ADHD symptoms.

While everyone intends to eat better and treat their body like a temple instead of a bin for junk food, turning this desire into reality can be immensely hard because the world of nutrition is very confusing and full of contradictions and disputes. We can cut through the smoke by dividing the optimal dietary advice into two groups -

universally accepted as beneficial and anecdotal opinions you can consider trying to see if they work for you.

Let's get started with the first group. The most commonly given advice for people with ADHD is to eat enough protein because the amino acids you get are the building blocks not only for every cell in the body but also for the neurotransmitters your brain desperately needs.[18]

Furthermore, if you are taking any sort of medication, you may see effects more quickly if you have a protein-heavy meal before taking your meds since the abundance of amino acids makes it easier for your meds to ramp up neurotransmitter production.

The second most common advice is to rule out vitamin and mineral deficiencies. Not because they are the underlying hidden cause for your ADHD but because they can mimic ADHD symptoms, leading to exacerbated side effects. The most common nutrients that you may not be getting enough of are iron, zinc, magnesium, vitamin D, vitamin B12, other vitamin B's, and omega 3s if you consume lots of ultra-processed foods (the typical Western diet).

You can correct the deficiency by supplementing in the beginning and gradually improving your diet to have sources high in the nutrients you were previously missing.

For example, magnesium and zinc can be found in dairy products and various types of nuts, and omega-3 fatty acids can be received from eggs or fatty fish like tuna, salmon, and sardines. Omega 3's, in particular, have been found to improve cognitive function, alertness, and memory in children and adults with ADHD.[19]

Getting nutrients from food is the preferable option because you know what you are getting, while with supplements, you have no guarantee of quality. The FDA has guidelines, but doesn't regulate the production of supplements, and there is always a profit motivation to reduce quality to increase how much money the company is getting.

Before all of that, you need to get officially tested because guessing in the dark is counterproductive, and you can't accurately assess precisely what your nutrient may be missing.

Thirdly, most nutritional experts with ADHD expertise agree you need to significantly curb or entirely eliminate quick carbohydrates and sugar from your diet. Quick carbs refer to foods like cookies, soda, fruit juice, sweets, pastries, bakery goods, candy, and any other source of carbohydrates that has high sugar, fructose, and other forms of sugar without many other nutrients and with a very low amount of fiber.[20]

Carbs are a powerful short-term energy source, but they spike your insulin, cause wild fluctuations in blood sugar levels, and inevitably lead to a total physical and mental crash after you get the initial energy spike. Think of the lethargy and brain fog after a huge meal at lunch, which makes your body beg for a nap. That's what many people consider a crash due to carbohydrates.

Having your mood, alertness, energy, and focus fluctuate wildly is highly disturbing, especially if you already struggle with all that, so we want to minimize the spikes as much as possible.

Unfortunately, eliminating sugar entirely from your diet will be very challenging unless you have a lot of money to spend on grocery shopping. Since it is highly addictive, most companies put sugar in their products, which is why sauces, ready-to-cook frozen meals, salad dressings, oatmeal, yogurts, granola bars, smoothies, and all sorts of other junk are all packed with sugar.

If your diet was previously very high in sugar, the solution isn't exactly to bounce toward the other extreme. There are diets that eliminate sugar almost entirely, like the keto and carnivore diets, but they are very expensive to maintain, highly restrictive, and hard to sustain if you are going out with people and having a social life. The biggest problem with highly restrictive regimes is the yo-yo effect. You force yourself to stay committed but eventually snap and go on an enormous binging episode for days or weeks, where you eventually fall back down to level one.

This doesn't mean going carnivore, keto, or any other rather restrictive diet doesn't have a time and place. If you are into strength training and cutting after a serious bulk, or you are under a medically supervised weight loss protocol with a large caloric deficit supported by supplementation, then go for it. Those diets can serve as a short-term solution where you teach your body not to rely on sugar so much.

However, for the average person, a more sustainable approach would be following the 80 to 20 principles. This simply means you have to make it a habit to eat healthy, nutrient-rich, and balanced meals 80% of the time - high-quality meat cuts, salads, nuts and seeds as snacks and toppings, fish and seafood multiple times a week, a wide variety of fruits and veggies, etc.

The remaining 20% you can save when you are going out with friends, having a date night with your partner or a prospective match, or when you are feeling horrible and need to numb the pain with your favorite snacks and treats. It is not perfect, but it is much easier to maintain.

Finally, one neglected but undoubtedly beneficial nutrition advice is to have systems in place so you can always quickly craft yourself some meal you'd enjoy, even if it's not perfect. While in reality, having three meals a day would be optimal, we all know that in the midst of a busy day, scheduling more than an hour in total for preparation and cooking is not feasible for most people. Just because you can't make it perfect every time doesn't mean you have to get angry and skip a meal altogether.

Personally, I have a huge list of recipes on sticky notes - ranging from easy to complicated. Whenever I feel down and drained, I pull out some of the easy ones. You may be tired, but you are never too tired not to make yourself oatmeal with seeds and fruits, a quick smoothie with five ingredients and protein powder, or a sandwich. If I haven't stocked the fridge, I order food online because paying a little more is worth it if I get to eat at all.

This is all for the common sense and universally beneficial advice that I highly doubt people will dispute. However, there is a whole other world of nutritional advice where people take nootropics (herbal supplements to enhance cognitive function), look into their gene history for potential hints on why they have ADHD, and try to correct malfunctions by hyper-dosing on vitamins, and all sorts of unorthodox nutritional trends.

You are your own human being, and you can do whatever you want. However, before you jump down some obscure nutritional rabbit hole, it should be said that just like everything else in life, the vast majority of the benefits you experience will come from sticking to the fundamentals - getting enough calories, protein, healthy fats, vitamins and minerals, and other essential nutrients, like omega 3s.

Trying alternative approaches is very attractive because they offer huge benefits compared to the effort you have to put in, but we both know this isn't realistic. No supplement, herbal extract, or plant compound will fix a crappy diet, so don't slack on that. What's equally important is that even a perfect diet will not fix your ADHD. It will make your symptoms better, but it won't make them disappear. Knowing this allows you to adjust your expectations and not feel crushed when your 12-week effort to eat healthier doesn't fundamentally change your life.

Perfection is not achievable, but you should still try to make progress towards a healthier life. Even a 20% improvement in your ADHD symptoms is a major victory that should be cherished and celebrated.

The Role of Medication in Treating ADHD

You can only know if medication will work for you or not after consulting with a medical professional and a licensed clinician. They are the only ones that can accurately choose what type of medication would best suit you and give you an appropriate dosage that can generate the most positive impact with the least side effects.

If you have a meeting scheduled and are looking for information before that, or have had a visit and want to learn more to better understand their purpose, we will cover it all.

ADHD brains are chronically deprived of sufficient stimulation and don't produce enough essential neurotransmitters like dopamine and norepinephrine. Most ADHD medications are stimulants designed to compensate for that.

They boost the production of neurotransmitters in your body and lift you towards a more optimal level. ADHD medications are specifically designed for people with the condition, and the chance for side effects is much larger if you are neurotypical.

This is why drugs like Adderall may have a calming effect on someone with ADHD when administered by a doctor, but when misused in the wrong dosage by neurotypicals, they may feel jittery, restless, and nauseous despite the slight boost in alertness.[21]

The craving for stimulation is why many undiagnosed men self-medicate with sugar, coffee, energy drinks, or other substances to help themselves function. In the absence of medication or highly stimulating activities, like working out, immersing yourself in a creative project, or doing what you feel passionate about, you feel a gap that needs to be filled so you can function normally.

Not all ADHD medications are the same. Some work as stimulants by releasing brain chemicals and improving neurotransmitter production, like Adderall. Other drugs, like Strattera, work on increasing the concentration of norepinephrine and dopamine in the prefrontal cortex without making you dependent on it compared to stimulants. Strattera and other similar medications can be equally effective in treating ADHD symptoms, and some opt in for them as they find the side effects more bearable compared to stimulants.

As with any other medication containing synthetic compounds, ADHD medications have side effects. The most common include trouble sleeping, loss of appetite, higher blood pressure, faster heart rate, stomachaches, headaches, and others.

What side effects you get will depend entirely on the drug you are taking, the dosage, and how your body responds. Two people can take the same dose of ADHD medication, and one can see an immense improvement with little setbacks, while the other may see only side effects and no positives, because each person's body is different.

Most people who take medications either don't experience much, if any, side effects, or the little problems that arise due to the ADHD drugs, like lowered appetite and higher blood pressure, are seen as a worthy trade-off for the positive impact they experience. For others who've tried various medications and doses and stopped them, the meds didn't work at all, didn't create a strong enough effect, the positive impact reduced over time, or they had other concerns like getting dependent on the medicine and having issues during a potential shortage.

Contrary to many sensational claims and loud critics, stimulant ADHD medications are not inherently addictive. On the contrary, taking ADHD medications in a supervised environment can actually reduce the chance of addictions and impulsive relapse into old dependencies because you are not chronically starved for stimulation.[22]

Although some people with ADHD feel the need to go to a higher dose, this is because the initial dose may not have been sufficiently high to get them the desired positive result. If your body gets used to the medication, the most common strategy is not to up the dosage but to have short periods where you go off meds so your body can stop adapting to the meds.

Whether you choose to take medications or not is a highly personal choice. Different people can respond to medications in vastly different ways.

Some people think you should give medication a chance at least once, simply because you can't make an informed choice on which way is preferable - with or without medication, without having personal and direct experience on both sides. I personally have seen many men with ADHD benefit from giving medication a try, at least for a short while, because it gives them the peace of mind and momentum to start building healthier habits and routines.

Other people believe there is nothing wrong with never trying, and it is a valid personal choice. You don't lose much if anything if you try. It's all up to you in the end.

If you decide to get medicated or at least try ADHD medications for a short while, you should speak only with a qualified medical professional who has the certifications to assess your needs and prescribe you an appropriate drug and dosage. Although tempting, stay away from any unofficial, off-store, and black-market options since you never know if the dosage is right and what actually goes into the final product.

Finally, before trying anything, you should know ADHD medications are not a cure nor a magic pill that will suddenly fix your ADHD symptoms. Most people who've tried meds describe it as being easier to stay focused, feeling less overwhelmed and anxious, being able to think more clearly, and having other positive impacts, but they still struggle with motivation, starting tasks, remembering important details, etc. It makes life easier, but it doesn't remove all obstacles in your way.

If you want to try using ADHD medications, it's helpful to think of them as assistance toward building a healthy life consisting of regular activity, balanced eating, abundant rest, and other healthy habits.

The boost it gives you is best used to take care of other issues that may be worsening your symptoms and to build habits, routines, and systems that support your neurodivergent brain.

For example, the improved alertness, calmness, and ability to focus a bit better can help you set up a calendar system with reminders and alarms for everything upcoming for the next 20 weeks, reducing how much you worry about appointments or forget and get angry at yourself. It can also help you finally clean up your home, giving you a new environment to work in, which increases motivation and reduces anxiety as the clutter is no longer overwhelming to your senses.

At the very beginning of my diagnosis, I was highly skeptical of any medication. Not only did I have an outdated and false perception of the side effects, but my masculine spirit screamed in protest at being dependent on a pill to lead an excellent life. I'm not using meds because they clash with other pre-existing health conditions I have, but over time, I grew up and realized using medications is not a sign of weakness.

Just like we use bikes instead of running to work, machines to clean the dishes and our clothes, and dumbbells to lift weights instead of using work, there is nothing wrong or shameful about making your life easier. After all, it makes life easier, but you still need to put in the effort to make it through.

Outsourcing Executive Dysfunction Issues With Outside Support

If you can afford it and there are options available nearby, there are various services that you can try that provide external assistance to better manage your ADHD. Depending on your budget, we can separate this into two categories.

The first is paid services from people who specialize in the treatment of ADHD. Personally, therapy has had the most profound change in my life, even if I was initially resistant to the treatment protocols and went in very skeptical of any change. What type of therapy you decide to do will depend on the biggest issues you are grappling with right now.

If you are an action-oriented problem-solver, then CBT could be a great fit. Struggling with acceptance of your condition is usually handled well with acceptance and commitment therapy (ACT). If your ADHD is combined with trauma, then psychoanalysis could be an excellent fit for you. Ask for recommendations from your primary health provider, and make sure it is feasible with your budget because the biggest benefits come from consistency with therapy.

Another popular option is ADHD coaching. Many people are confused about the nuance between coaching and therapy. Basically, therapists are more qualified because they need multiple degrees and certification by the state. Coaches, on the other hand, only need to go through a course that isn't always accredited. Of course, there are reputable organizations supervising quality, so if you want to try with a coach, look for people with CHADD, PAAC, ADDCA, or ADHD-centered certification by the ICF.

While therapists primarily help you treat, heal, and improve mental health disorders and their symptoms, coaches are more focused on positive psychology and personal growth. Therapists help to resolve serious problems, while coaches offer advice on how to lead your everyday life to make the most out of it. In particular, ADHD coaches specialize in helping you better manage symptoms and the mental, emotional, social, and professional consequences and differences that stem from those symptoms.

They can keep you accountable and assist you in finding strategies and tools to better manage your daily life. Furthermore, they can be of great assistance in helping you identify your goals, set a system through which you plan to achieve them, and keep an eye regularly on the progress you are making to achieve those goals.

Those are two of the primary options that would be suitable for most people with ADHD, but your needs may be different, and you may have a hyper-specific issue you wish to address. For instance, professional organizers are people who can assist you in developing easy-to-maintain and sustainable organizational systems to free up time and reduce clutter. This can be very helpful if your primary issue is the chaos in your home and the lack of a proper digital system for work and side projects.

As we previously discussed, many people with ADHD struggle to find a suitable career. This is why if you struggle with professional orientation, then you can consult with a career guide. Working with a career guide involves exploring your interests, personality traits, and strengths in order to offer a wide variety of potential opportunities you can try. Career guides cannot only help you better understand what you want but also help you along the way by keeping you on track toward your career goals and crafting an action plan toward those aims.

One final option to consider is social skills training. This can sound counterintuitive because you'd assume humans should inherently know how to socialize and productively interact in settings with coworkers, acquaintances, friends, family, dates, and partners, but we both know it isn't true. The training most often involves personalized exercises and drills in a controlled environment to measure improvement, as well as routines that you can practice by yourself.

The benefit of paid options is that there is some guarantee of quality, and most often, they are set up by businesses or agencies that you could check the reviews of online. Aside from therapy and potentially coaching, you don't need specialized services unless you have a persistent problem you can't resolve, no matter what. Such services often provide convenience, accountability, and a clear structure to build a habit you previously didn't have, but they are not essential for most people.

Thankfully, not every external support for ADHD has to cost money.

One of the easiest ways to get work done when paralyzed with in-action, procrastinating, and unable to contain your impulses and attention is to get an ADHD work buddy. This could be a friend, family member, co-worker with similar issues, or a total stranger you find on ADHD forums, Discord servers, etc.

Having an ADHD buddy, also called body doubling, involves doing work in the presence of another person. They may work alongside you, independently do their own projects, or just be present. The presence of another person can motivate us to stick to the task and may reduce distractibility and hyperactivity. This strategy is a hit-or-miss. For some, it works like a charm, while others just continue to get distracted despite being in the presence of someone else. To know where you fall, you will have to try it out for yourself.

Another way to find assistance is by joining an ADHD support group.

Before you shrug this one off, hold on a second. I know what you are thinking. As a man, I know how the typical group dynamic we are used to is one of constant bantering, joking around, mockery of one another, and other funny but totally immature topics.

ADHD support groups are not group therapy. You don't have to share deeply personal and intimate moments of your life with strangers. The point is to show up, see how others are going through the same, share how you experience similar pains and offer some advice, or be silent if you don't feel comfortable. Just showing up is enough to reap some benefits since you are very likely to learn something useful about yourself through the lens of others.

Feeling understood and validated by people who truly get what you are going through because they face similar challenges can be a wonderful way to better understand your condition and manage your symptoms through community support. ADHD support groups can be both digital networks of people or real-life organizations. You can opt-in for both depending on your schedule, availability, and preferences.

If you are interested in ADHD support groups in real life, then research if your town happens to have any. ADHD support groups don't necessarily have to be based in real life, and sometimes, geographical differences and incompatibility in schedules make it nearly impossible. Online meetings, forums, and chat rooms are a convenient alternative. There are whole forums dedicated to ADHD, specifically women and mothers with ADHD, and there are also huge communities on platforms like Reddit or Discord.

Chapter 5

Taking Control of Emotional Dysregulation – Overcoming Anger Issues, Mood Swings, and Strong Emotions

When people think of ADHD, they associate it with zoning out, procrastination, always being late, and constantly forgetting even simple things. The mainstream spotlight is almost entirely focused on the productivity challenges arising from ADHD, not emotional ones.

Uncontrollable anger, irritation refusing to go down, sudden mood swings, and fluctuations in how you feel are all symptoms of emotional dysregulation - one of the most underlooked ADHD symptoms.

This chapter will shed light on how emotional dysregulation may be affecting your life, before diving into strategies you can implement to better control strong emotions, stop impulsivity from running wild in social settings, and better communicate your feelings and thoughts to others.

How To Manage and Control Anger, Impulsivity, And Strong Emotions

The relationship between emotions and masculinity is very complex. We are not supposed to be very emotional because this is seen by many as a sign of weakness and immaturity. Shoving emotions in your mind's locker is the way to go for most men.

Even if society is modernizing and gender norms are becoming more lenient, this seems to be one of the cornerstones of masculinity that isn't going away. After all, if you had it imprinted in you thousands of times, a few liberal messages would not be changing much.

This wouldn't be a huge problem if you could just remove emotions and decide not to feel them so they disappear. But emotions do not work like this. They are felt for a reason, and your mind refuses to eliminate them because of their purpose. Many men make the mistake that since they are not feeling much, they must have become less emotional. The truth is, they have just become very good at staying out of touch with how they feel. This is very risky because, one way or another, emotions build up and will eventually explode on someone or over something.

Have you ever snapped on a partner? Have you gotten extremely angry over someone's mistake toward you? Or did you feel very aggravated and spiteful toward the people around you, making nasty assumptions about them in your mind? Intense emotions don't need to have a social component. You can be intensely angry at yourself over something or just exasperated and in a horrible mood for no particular reason.

After all, emotional dysregulation is not the same for every male. Not all of us descend into an anger episode at the slightest inconvenience. It can also be very subtle and mostly felt internally without a direct outburst into the real world.

We can holistically address emotional dysregulation with mindset adjustment, preventative measures, and on-the-ground strategies you can immediately implement.

There are two ways I like to think of my emotions.

The first is to acknowledge how short-lasting they are once you fully allow yourself to experience them. Think of how many times you felt miserable while sick, extremely pained during a long workout, or overwhelmingly angry at someone only to feel normal the next day. Emotions are messengers; they make us feel, and then they naturally subdue us. Whenever I feel strong and intense emotions, I remind myself that this, too, will pass.

The second mindset adjustment goes hand in hand with the first - emotions don't have to lead to actions.

As people with ADHD, we experience lots of intense emotions, sudden urges, and impulsive thoughts, so our perception of the link between emotions and action can get blurred. There is this huge misconception that you shouldn't be acting out on negative emotions, like irritation, anger, and spite, so to be safe, you need to shut off emotions altogether. The right balance is feeling emotions but deciding whether to act on them or not.

This is how you should think of emotions, but I realize just knowing the optimal way to interact with your emotions will not be effective if you feel overwhelmed by them at a given moment. The whole point of intense emotions is that they shut off rational thinking altogether. You can't stop experiencing intense emotions altogether, but you can reduce how strongly they hit you out of nowhere by getting more in touch with how you are feeling on a regular basis.

Below, we will have a whole section on meditation and how mindfulness can improve your mood, emotion control, and awareness of feelings and thoughts. An equally powerful way to stay in touch with your emotions is to journal. Personally, I like to do a complete brain dump every few days where I write down all the dozens of things that have bothered me. Irrational or not. Small or huge problems. It doesn't matter as long as you get all of them out there.

No matter what type of journaling you do, the very act of writing them all down on a piece of paper is hugely important. By seeing them written on paper, you create distance and begin to recognize they are just transient emotions and thoughts, not something that defines you or you have to act upon. It also helps you to better conceptualize and understand what you are feeling, to begin with, turning uncomfortable feelings at the back of your mind into specific negative emotions that have a particular cause and reason to exist.

Journaling can also have the opposite effect. It allows you to connect to more mild, mellow, and not easily recognizable emotions and sentiments you hold.

Ones that had remained buried inside for so long because your natural response to feeling was to disassociate what made you emotional. Before the resistance to this new self-awareness grows, recognize that suppression does not work. You need to know what you are dealing with to manage it effectively. Burying it alive will only make your emotions eventually burst out, angry you had them locked up in the ground for so long.

There are hundreds of ways you can journal. If you are an absolute beginner, you can start with free journaling. Just a piece of paper, a stack of papers, a notebook, or anything else that can do the job and begin writing everything on your mind, no matter if it's related or not to one another. Do this for 20 minutes at a time.

After doing it a few times, you can narrow down and pick one source of negative emotions or troubling thoughts and look into it deeper by writing out everything you know about it and making interpretations.

Still, you can't always sit down and journal for 15 straight minutes. Fortunately, you can still get some of the benefits if you start to feel yourself getting heated and overwhelmed with intense emotions. Pull out a voice recording app, start the recording, and just start talking. List every single thing that annoys you, pisses you off, and gets you angry and mad. Irrational or not, it doesn't matter. I've done it countless times and, in many cases, deleted the recording right after.

We all experience strong emotions, like exasperation and anger. There is nothing wrong with that. It becomes a problem when we lose control, and we lose control when the amount of what we feel becomes more than our mind can handle in a given moment. With this technique, you can get an instant outlet and reduce some of the pressure.

Using Meditation To Improve Mood, Emotional Awareness, and Impulse Control

Just as you can train your body with strength training, your heart with cardio, and your athletic skills with intentional practice, you can also train your mind and emotional control with meditation.

I used to shrug off meditation, not taking it seriously. I'd do it once or twice a week for 8 to 10 minutes, but most weeks, I'd skip it altogether. It was only once I put it as my sole priority and gave it a chance for six months that I got almost life-altering benefits.

I know Buddhist practices and philosophy can be confusing and overwhelming in their requirements, so I will keep it simple. You don't have to become a literal monk to reap benefits from meditation.

Think of meditation and being mindful as a non-judgemental observation of the world and your thoughts, emotions, and internal experiences. You focus inward and observe. If something arises, like a thought or an emotion, you acknowledge it before letting go and returning your attention back to your anchor. Most often, the anchor is your breathing since it is the easiest to spot.

Personally, mindfulness exercises and extended meditation have been the most effective ways to reduce my inattention, impulsivity, and mood swings. This is because they trained directly in the areas where I was the weakest due to my ADHD.

I used to automatically respond to any impulse and negative emotional urge, but regular mindfulness exercises drilled into me how I can acknowledge a craving without giving in to it. Meditation slowed me down, leaving time to catch up with my emotions and acknowledge them without letting them define me. Inattention made my attention wander off, and I'd get off track entirely, but with meditation, you practice over and over again how to return your attention despite getting distracted.

Meditation is not a cure for your ADHD. It is not a replacement for therapy, being healthy, and working with professionals. Still, it is the most accessible and direct way to train your brain to compensate for ADHD symptoms anywhere, whenever you want, and for how much you want without limitations.

Best of all, since mindfulness has entered the mainstream, the amount of research and clinical studies backing its usefulness has only grown larger and larger.[23]

Still, even if you know the benefits, you may not want to do meditation. The most common complaint I hear is about how boring meditation is. I have to admit, sitting down and focusing on yourself isn't very exciting compared to browsing social media. Even if that's the case, there are ways to make meditation less boring.

First, you can do meditation after taking a very hot shower after a cold plunge, right after a strength-based or cardio workout, or just after drinking your cup of coffee. All those activities stimulate the production of neurotransmitters naturally, making you more likely to feel less agitated and starved for boredom. Second, you can try meditating with your eyes open, so that one of your senses is more stimulated.

Finally, meditation becomes much less boring if you make it last more than 15 minutes. Meditating above this time will also resolve the second most commonly heard complaint about meditation not working for you.

This feeling of not doing anything beneficial and suffering from boredom is most common in the warm-up phase, which is in the first 15 to 20 minutes. You can't judge a four-mile run based on how you feel in the first half a mile, right? Similarly, if your brain is used to rapidly bouncing thoughts all over the place and constant stimulation, it will need some time to adapt. If you push through this "warm-up," you are more likely to see noticeable benefits and feel meditation is less painful and boring.

The Classic Meditation Practice

This is a beginner-friendly meditation drill you can try for yourself. Start with 5 minutes if you have never done it before. Here are the steps you can follow:

1. **Pick the right location** - Find someplace quiet to sit down. The temperature should be comfortable and not cause distraction. Outside noises should be minimized as well. If you intend to make it a habit, it's preferable to choose a place you can frequently visit and associate with that meditation practice.

2. **Get comfortable** - Once you sit down, straighten your spine and get comfortable. Sit straight on your own with crossed legs, or lean lightly against something for support. Avoid lying down since a straight spine keeps you more engaged and alert.

3. **Turn inward and find your anchor** - Close your eyes, and turn toward your inner sensations. It can be hard in the beginning, living a busy, always-on-the-go life where you are always focusing inwards, but try to look within and find an anchor. You could choose from many inner sensations, but trying to follow your breath is the easiest to follow.

4. **Focus on the anchor** - Life may be busy, complicated, and overwhelming. I'm not asking you to forget about it all and blissfully ignore it, but put it aside for the next few minutes. The only thing that matters is your breathing now. Focus all your attention on it.

5. **Sense the upcoming emotions and rumination** - In the beginning, it will be easy. You can feel the lightness of the air, the slight tingling you feel, the way your body naturally gives way, and your chest expands. But, gradually, you will start to feel burdened and distracted.

6. **Acknowledge and let go** - Your head is not supposed to be blank. Never ignore what you feel and think. Acknowledge any thoughts, emotions, and anything in between that tries to occupy your attention. Give it your attention for a second without any shame, then let it go and return to your anchor.

7. **Repeat and return** - Your focus is not supposed to be unwavering. No matter how much you try, some thoughts and emotions will suddenly or subtly pull you toward

them. The point is to gradually learn to realize how you've gotten distracted and return to the sensation. Zoning out is not a failure if you return back to your anchor.

Don't just stare at the instructions and think about trying it out sometime in the future. Put the book down, set an alarm for 5 to 8 minutes if you are a beginner, and do the exercise yourself. This way, you will get your first taste of mindfulness and more easily make it a habit to take action instead of only observing.

Integrating Meditation and Mindfulness In Your Everyday Life

As long as you make an effort to stick to the rules, there is no wrong way to meditate. The guided meditation you just read about and, hopefully, tried for yourself is one of endless variations. Some people meditate with their eyes open to reduce anxiety, feel more stimulated, and not get sleepy. Others feel too restless in one place and do mindful walks where they fall into a rhythm and use the grounding sensation of their feet touching the floor as an anchor.

If you are used to constantly working, drowning yourself in stimulation with music, social media, TV, video games, and other sources, and always moving around from one place to another, then meditation will feel somewhat uncomfortable and alien. After all, it asks you to do something you would never do otherwise. Sit down in silence, slow down, turn inward, and get in touch with your thoughts and feelings.

If you are serious about trying meditation, you don't have to become extreme and go into days-long silent retreats where you do nothing but meditate and pretend to be a monk. Usually, meditating for 15 to 20 minutes a day is enough to get the benefits.

Here is a very simple structure to get started:

1. **Week 1** - 2 minutes each day.
2. **Week 2 and 3** - 5 minutes each day.
3. **Week 4** - 8 minutes each day.
4. **Week 5 and 6** - 10 minutes each day.
5. **Week 7 to 10** - 15 minutes each day.
6. **Week 11 to 15** - 18 minutes each day.
7. **Week 16 and onward** - 20 minutes each day.

This is just an example of a meditation plan you can follow. If you progress more quickly or slowly, you can make your own. The longer you meditate daily, the more likely you are to have days you don't feel motivated or in the right headspace. This is why there is more time in between each progression.

You can do only 5 minutes daily, even if you aim for 10 or 15. Even if it's below your previous record, doing some form of meditation each day is still successful because you are building up the habit.

As always, the strategies we've discussed so far in the book on habit building can help make meditation part of your daily life. Using apps and software with guided meditation can make it more convenient and externalize the effort of setting up and thinking about how you'd approach each session. Stacking meditation with another habit can make it more likely to stick, so you can do it after your morning routine, workout, or any other habit.

Lastly, don't feel ashamed and over-complicate it. Just because you struggle to sit still and do nothing but focus on your breathing doesn't make you any less of a man. Standing meditation doesn't work for many men, so they focus on other meditation drills, like mindful walking. Even if one exercise doesn't work, you can always try another. Experiment and see for yourself.

Seeing The Full Picture - Comorbidities and Mental Health

Sometimes, nothing works, no matter how much you try to get your emotions in control. You feel numb and apathetic most of the time, but once in a while, you get overwhelmed with fury for not feeling anything. You feel chronically anxious and paranoid, making you more aggravated and likely to lash out at other people.

In short, it feels like you are trying to solve a puzzle when there is a missing piece.

This could be because you got your ADHD diagnosed, but there may be other skeletons in the closet - other mental health disorders that remain undiagnosed.[24]

Very often, ADHD doesn't dance alone. It comes with, or the symptoms of ADHD directly cause, other conditions, like anxiety disorders, depressive episodes, BPD, and other conditions. Furthermore, ADHD significantly increases the chance of learning struggles as a child and conflicts with parents, family, and peers, and this can lead to traumatic events.

I know you have the urge to ignore this advice, to pretend there is nothing wrong with you because admitting to mental health issues feels like a personal failure, and you'd honestly prefer to suffer in the shadows than admit failure in the light. Personally, I'd prefer to be safe than sorry and get myself checked for other disorders through therapy. What you do is up to you, but I will ask you one simple question - what would be more helpful?

To make a large display of your masculine strength, self-reliance, and perseverance despite the potential for additional problems is your automatic response to what you have done thousands of times before and what society has imprinted on you as the default setting. But sit back and take a moment to ask if this will really make your life better. It's an absurdly simple question but one we don't ask often enough.

Being on your own and continuing the way you are offers some benefits. The passive sense of accomplishment, how you are managing it all by yourself, and the mild comfort of being strong and resilient to everything. But this macho display of power is not enough to fix the slump you feel 4 out of 7 days in the week, the racing thoughts and overwhelming stress when you need to make a presentation at work, or the uncontrollable mood swings negatively affecting your relationships with the people closest to you.

No one denies self-reliance doesn't have some worth, but at the end of the day, you have to ask yourself - is feeling good on your own better than stepping up and addressing other problems you could have?

Coping with ADHD alone will not be enough if there is a second culprit hiding at the crime scene. Only by having a full picture of everything going on in your mind can you effectively start building up habits, systems, support networks, and your life in a way that helps you to combat the challenges you are facing.

Chapter 6

Relationships And ADHD - How To Communicate Effectively And Preserve Intimacy

Communication is not the biggest talent for us with ADHD. We stumble on our words, interrupt others without realizing it, go on tangents about seemingly unrelated topics that are connected only because of our far-fetched logic, and react with intense emotion instead of reason, even when not threatened.

This chapter will offer practical strategies you can add to your everyday life to navigate everyday conversations more effectively and clearly express your thoughts and emotions to prevent conflict, tension, and disagreements from turning into full-blown conflicts and damaging fights.

Why Communication Matters So Much

We all know communicating well with others matters, but for most it is not a priority to work on. If you fall into this group, I wouldn't blame you. This defeatist mindset comes from the wrong belief that social skills are innate. You either have them, or you don't. You are either the charismatic, smooth, and socially popular one in the room or a weird and awkward outsider. However, this couldn't be further from the truth.

Social skills, just like any other skill, can be worked upon and improved. When you think of great speeches, you likely think of Winston Churchill during WWII or Steve Jobs inspiring college students in graduation ceremonies, but both of them struggled immensely for years before developing their craft.

You can still make significant progress even if you don't become the greatest public speaker or private conversationalist. Communicating effectively is not an all-or-nothing art. Every time you ask an additional question, instead of averting the topic in a random direction, position yourself toward the person you are talking with and make a conscious effort to look at them once or twice, and take a few seconds before answering, you've made progress.

Clearly articulating your thoughts and feelings is helpful in all settings, but honesty and transparency are the lifeblood of any romantic relationship. It can be hard to see, but ineffective communication with your partner can trigger a domino effect that goes out of control and harms many other aspects of your relationship without realizing it.

For example, if you own up to your mistakes, fully open up about how you are struggling, and show an intentional commitment to be better, it is much easier for your partner not to get upset and angry with you. This simple act can make them more understanding and compassionate, rather than aggravated and passive-aggressive, which can be the difference between talking it out or going down a negative spiral that ends up in shouting.

A shouting match and a heated exchange are horrible experiences for both of you. The trouble doesn't end there. If you miscommunicate, the other person will feel lonely, unheard, and ignored, making them less likely to seek physical comfort, more aggravated when you are having a normal conversation, and less likely to make nice gestures for you in the upcoming hours or even days. The feeling of unresolved conflict and tension is not visible but can still be a massive burden on any relationship.

How To Effectively Communicate With Your Partner and Loved Ones

Impulsivity, emotional dysregulation, and inattention create unique obstacles when communicating with the people you care most about. However, just because you struggle now doesn't mean you can not make future conversations more clear, constructive, and properly articulated. Here is how you can do it.

Work With Intention

We have so many conversations each day that it's natural to go with the flow and respond automatically without much thought. However, improvement begins with an effort to be observant and intentionally look for context in the environment and the body to better grasp what is happening.

A person's tone of voice, facial features, gestures, and body language can say a lot about their behavior. For instance, going on 20 minutes about a passion project to a friend is great, but you may want to give them the floor if they are really feeling down and need to share.

One Goal at a Time

Conversations can be very overwhelming because they are very dynamic. A person's talking, making odd facial expressions, waving their hands in all kinds of mystical movements, and giving many other cues.

This is why it's only feasible to focus solely on a single social skill at a time. For instance, you can try to look into the mouth or eyes of a person to focus better, give yourself a few seconds before replying to let all the information sink in, and even ask, "I think I got the general idea. Can you please repeat the main points just in case I missed something?" If you think you missed something.

Own up When You Fall Short in a Conversation

If you own up to your shortcomings, they become armor instead of a weapon used against you. When in a conversation, even if you enjoy it greatly, you may find yourself zoning out. In such cases, the person on the other side very likely notices and feels a bit neglected and ignored, so just nodding and trying to catch up with the whole picture is not working for either of you.

Be honest, admit you couldn't follow through, make a joke about it even, apologize, and ask for them to repeat one or two details. Owning up to your problems shows commitment to a conversation.

Focus On Becoming a Better Listener

Most people think of talking as the most enjoyable part of a conversation. You share what matters to you and steal the spotlight. Listening is seen as a boring and passive role. However, it requires persistent attention to one person, pondering upon their words and what they mean to say, and gently asking them questions to keep them going.

By switching to listening mode, it becomes much easier to avoid excessively talking, interrupting, and drifting into unrelated topics because you have more scarcity in the amount of time available to speak.

Listening is an excellent way to capture impulsivity, not because you will suddenly shut up forever, but because your impulses to speak out will come out in the form of questions, which is much less intrusive and disrupting than taking charge of the conversation.

Change Your Hobbies

Earlier, we talked about how the environment and your habits can significantly help you build certain skills because they offer lots of room for practice.

I became excellent at speaking to people after doing competitive debating for five years because I had to say as much as possible in a small time frame and then listen to others. I'm not saying you necessarily need to pick debating. There are also public speaking, improv acting, toastmasters, storytelling clubs, or just about any club with a social element where you can speak freely. The more your time off aligns with practicing on the side, the better you become.

Strategies for Effective Conflict Resolution

No matter how much you take care of yourself, communicate well with your partner, family, friends, and loved ones, and keep up with emotional dysregulation exercises, conflicts will happen. Still, even if tension and disagreements are inevitable, you control how large they become. Life is full of small fires. It is up to you not to stop them from existing but to prevent them from burning the whole place down.

I found that trying to use my mind to get myself to calm down didn't really work because my mind tends to tunnel vision and become stubborn due to the intensity of emotions I feel at times.

If I am arguing with someone, then I'd simply ask them for a 5-minute interruption, get my legs to work, and leave the room. This way, I can get myself to calm down by staying by myself for a bit only by moving myself to another room, which is something most people can make themselves do more easily than changing how they think in the moment.

I do this because if you get into an argument with your partner or family member, the more uninterrupted time you spend on it will only grow worse. You will say your thoughts. They will say theirs, and both parties are bound to feel that the other is not listening because they don't concede, while the other side doesn't concede because they are defensive. It's a clear negative spiral that gets worse the more attacked and unheard you feel, triggering more intense emotions and responses.

When I disagree with my partner and feel heated, I say, "Give me 5 minutes," and just get out of the room. It is a bit sudden and awkward, but I'd take that any day to exploding on a person I love. I can't stop my emotions and everything I am feeling at the moment. But I can much more easily get my body to move, and it allows me to enter an environment without immediate triggers where I can calm down and let the emotions grow less intense.

There are many other ways to play around with your physiology to calm yourself and subdue emotions. My other two personal favorites are cold plunges and the physiological sigh. I know you can't take an ice-cold bath when feeling impulsive, pent up, and highly emotional, but you can get in the sink and wash your face with very cold water for at least a minute. It is not a miraculous fix, but it will help you to calm down and reduce the intensity of your emotions. It works like a reset button for me.

The physiological sigh is even more accessible and easy to do. All you need to do is take a short inhale, then take a second inhale to really fill your lungs, and then follow it up with an intentionally slow exhale that takes longer to do than your inhale.

A long exhale activates your vagus nerve, sending a signal to the parasympathetic nervous system responsible for stress, impulse, and strong emotion management. Do this for 15 to 20 reps, and you will feel slightly better. It is even better if you practice it every day, like by setting up an alarm every two hours to do one set of it.[25]

What physiological strategy you implement depends on what works for you. I've had people mention how they do a strength training session or go for a run whenever they get very angry or aggravated over something. Others begin to walk around at a fast pace while their fingers are tightly squeezing a grip-strengthening toy.

This can work if you are getting angry while texting or after a confrontation when you need to calm down, but breathwork is the most accessible and easy-to-use tool in the heat of the moment.

All of this works because emotions need an outlet.

You can acknowledge them and try to let go by being mindful, but this will not work in all cases, especially if what you are going through is relatively intense. By working with the physical aspect of your body, you give them an outlet and bypass the more emotional part of your brain. After all, when you feel impulsive and emotionally volatile, it is very hard to overcome the mind by using cognitive tricks since your mind is not cooperative. This is why what usually works best is tapping into a different pathway.

Telling Your Partner About ADHD, Accepting The Condition, and Navigating ADHD-Specific Challenges

If any of the advice above had to prepare you for something, it is for the time when you tell your partner you have ADHD.

This conversation is non-negotiable, and it must happen, even if you must absolutely delay the announcement for some time. This is because ADHD takes its toll on a relationship - the constant interruptions making a person feel ignored, forgetting big dates and meaningful anniversaries, hyper-focusing on projects and not paying enough attention to your partner, struggling at work due to executive dysfunction and eating up time at home to finish instead of spending it with your partner. You can probably make the list even larger.

The words you use are up to you because you know your partner best. However, there are two essential parts you have to include. First, you have to share the full context of the condition. Having ADHD is not just some minor issues with attention, self-control, and impulsivity, but a very real neurodevelopmental condition recognized by every reputable medical institution in the world. If you wish your partner to take it seriously, to accommodate, and offer compassion, then you must take it seriously yourself.

Second, there must be a balance between asking for understanding and forgiveness and promising to be responsible and work on it yourself as well.

Before the announcement, your partner may have felt exhausted, confused, and lonely because they see themselves as the only one responsible and the only person who's willing to put in the effort. The struggles you had communicating well, remembering important events, keeping up with your part of the house effort, and others felt like a personal failing or a sign you didn't love them enough. Showing there is another reason can be deeply comforting because it means you didn't intentionally hurt them. In a way, you are both victims.

However, this is not enough for most people. Temporary relief must come with a commitment to be better in the future.

You don't want to only point the spotlight toward another culprit responsible for the crime, but make sure the crime doesn't repeat again. Struggling to do your cleaning and home duties doesn't make you lazy and irresponsible anymore, but it's not an excuse to stop trying to make it work. Quite the contrary, now that both of you know the underlying problem, there are even fewer excuses because it is easier to find appropriate solutions.

This rule applies to anything that happens in the future that leads to friction, conflict, and fighting, like seeing their message and thinking you'd replied but you actually didn't, forgetting to do your cleaning duties, falling behind at work due to executive dysfunction and projecting your frustration on them, hyperfocusing on projects and not paying enough attention to your partner, or losing interest and zoning out when getting intimate.

No matter the situation, you do two things. First, avoid the extremes. Do not let your partner or anyone else deny you have ADHD, and it is entirely your personal failure and character responsible for what happened. Similarly, you don't want to go the other extreme and blame your ADHD entirely for your problems. It contributes to the problems you face, making life harder and more difficult to navigate, but you have some control and freedom to improve it and work around it.

Second, you focus your attention and mental energy on making sure it doesn't happen again, or it doesn't happen in the same way in the future. For example, did you forget to plan something for your anniversary or to do your home duties? It's fine to take a few moments and just be sad, but most of your energy should be going on how this will not happen again - by setting yourself multiple reminders so you can't forget no matter what.

Underneath this approach is one very simple question - is what you are doing helpful? Trying to calculate the exact percentage for which your ADHD is responsible in any given situation will drive you mad. Instead, offer a genuine apology whenever your partner was justifiably hurt by your actions, even if you didn't intend to hurt them, make a commitment to be better and focus all your energy on improving.

You won't fix your ADHD, but you can definitely make significant improvements in how you manage the condition, and for many partners, the very act of trying your best to be better is enough to adore and respect you.

Conclusion

You are running a marathon. Your heavy steps are pounding the pavement one after another. You feel on the verge of stopping with a mind that can't help but wonder, "How many more miles do I have to do?"

Before this book, you were running the marathon of your life with an overwhelmingly heavy backpack. However, this book is not a miracle. Just reading about your condition and the roadmap to improvement didn't cut the backpack from your shoulders. It only showed you how to unzip the backpack, throw away some of the weight, and reduce the burden you need to carry.

Working with ADHD means aiming to make your load lighter, not trying to rip apart the backpack altogether. But, for any of that to happen, you must take action. Reading the entire book was only step one. Now you have to put this knowledge into practice.

What you have read in this book may have been motivating, inspiring, and energizing, giving you new hope and desire for improvement, but it will die if you stay idle. Motivation is short-lived and fleeting, but you can use it to create momentum. You now possess a small ignition spark, but it is up to you to turn it into a blazing fire.

I bet you are overwhelmed. After dozens of pages, what precisely should you try to implement first? Let's simplify what your action plan should be to avoid action paralysis.

This book is not a one-time read in the afternoon. It is a mini encyclopedia of steps to improve your life. Reading it once gets you a general understanding of ADHD and the best strategies. Returning to it when you have a specific problem is where the real treasure lies.

Pick one area in life where you struggle the most - self-esteem and acceptance, career growth, productivity and getting work done, staying healthy and taking care of yourself, and communication and emotion control in relationships. Rate each one from 1 to 10.

If you can't properly assess the score, list the most common problems you experience in each area to make the final scoring more accurate. Pick only the single most urgent area for improvement. How much free time you have doesn't matter. The more you have, the more you can dedicate to improving more quickly.

Once you narrow it down to one area, you need to pick intentional actions, habits, and systems you can put your effort towards. If you are balancing a 9/5 on top of other hobbies, having a social life, and other responsibilities, then pick only a single piece of advice from the book and implement it without doing anything else. If you have more free time, say a few hours a day, you can pick two. Don't go overboard and do more than two at a time.

For example, if working outside of your 9/5 for career growth is your biggest priority, and you struggle with distractibility and inattention, then you can pick two exercises - meditation and time blocking as your primary tools. Your beginner goal would be 8 minutes of meditation two times a day, and you will only care to do that. To get yourself to work, you will put a 30-minute timer before every work session to create a sense of urgency.

You've spent your whole life, or most of your life, not doing the strategies you've just chosen to start, so you need to give it time. As we previously discussed, your mind is ego-defensive. It prefers familiar and comfortable actions even if they are not optimal for making the most out of your life. Changing yourself will take weeks, months, and even years. You don't chisel a statue out of the mold in a few days.

The simple golden rule is - if you didn't put it as your utmost priority to which you intentionally pay attention, does the strategy, action, and habit remain in your everyday life for at least four days of the week?

For example, you've been meditating for six weeks straight with only three days of missing the habit, and when you start to focus on working out, you barely meditate once a week. This means you didn't practice for a long enough time. Get back to point one and repeat until it becomes second nature.

I know you feel discomfort by this idea because the perfectionist in you claims you can get quicker by trying multiple things. Unfortunately, the perfectionist whisper in your mind is selling you an illusion. Either you get guaranteed results slowly, through trial and error, continuous setbacks, and regression, but perseverance despite everything, you try to do everything at once, get overwhelmed, and stop altogether.

Life rarely changes through a sudden and life-altering transformation where everything just starts working where it previously didn't. Slow and steady wins the race. You already have the knowledge, so all that remains is to put in the effort.

Pick an action, and let's get started.

Get Your Bonus Audiobook & Ebook: Overcoming Procrastination with ADHD

This audiobook will help you learn specific neurodivergent friendly techniques to overcome with procrastination.

To get your copy scan the QR code below.

References

1. Gallagher AM;De Lisi R;Holst PC;McGillicuddy-De Lisi AV;Morely M;Cahalan C; "Gender Differences in Advanced Mathematical Problem Solving." *Journal of Experimental Child Psychology*, U.S. National Library of Medicine, pubmed.ncbi.nlm.nih.gov/10666324/. Accessed 23 Nov. 2023.

2. Singh, Ajay, et al. "Overview of Attention Deficit Hyperactivity Disorder in Young Children." *Health Psychology Research*, U.S. National Library of Medicine, 13 Apr. 2015, www.ncbi.nlm.nih.gov/pmc/articles/PMC4768532/.

3. Berenson, Kathy R, et al. "Rejection Sensitivity and Disruption of Attention by Social Threat Cues." *Journal of Research in Personality*, U.S. National Library of Medicine, 1 Dec. 2009, www.ncbi.nlm.nih.gov/pmc/articles/PMC2771869/.

4. Katzman, Martin A, et al. "Adult ADHD and Comorbid Disorders: Clinical Implications of a Dimensional Approach." *BMC Psychiatry*, U.S. National Library of Medicine, 22 Aug.

2017, www.ncbi.nlm.nih.gov/pmc/articles/PMC5567978/#:~:text=Several%20studies%20have%20suggested%20that,have%20comorbid%20ADHD%20%5B77%5D.

5. Zulauf, Courtney A, et al. "The Complicated Relationship between Attention Deficit/Hyperactivity Disorder and Substance Use Disorders." *Current Psychiatry Reports*, U.S. National Library of Medicine, Mar. 2014, www.ncbi.nlm.nih.gov/pmc/articles/PMC4414493/.

6. Fuermaier, Anselm B M, et al. "ADHD at the Workplace: ADHD Symptoms, Diagnostic Status, and Work-Related Functioning." *Journal of Neural Transmission (Vienna, Austria : 1996)*, U.S. National Library of Medicine, July 2021, www.ncbi.nlm.nih.gov/pmc/articles/PMC8295111/.

7. Abdelnour, Elie, et al. "ADHD Diagnostic Trends: Increased Recognition or Overdiagnosis?" *Missouri Medicine*, U.S. National Library of Medicine, 2022, www.ncbi.nlm.nih.gov/pmc/articles/PMC9616454/.

8. Roselló, Belén, et al. "Empirical Examination of Executive Functioning, ADHD Associated Behaviors, and Functional Impairments in Adults with Persistent ADHD, Remittent ADHD, and without ADHD." *BMC Psychiatry*, U.S. National Library of Medicine, 24 Mar. 2020, www.ncbi.nlm.nih.gov/pmc/articles/PMC7092442/.

9. Juárez Olguín, Hugo, et al. "The Role of Dopamine and Its Dysfunction as a Consequence of Oxidative Stress." *Oxidative Medicine and Cellular Longevity*, U.S. National Library of Medicine, 2016, www.ncbi.nlm.nih.gov/pmc/articles/PMC4684895/.

10. Barkley, Russell A., Murphy, Kevin R., Fischer, Mariellen (2008). ADHD in Adults: What the Science Says (pp 171–175). New York, Guilford Press.

11. Hofmann, Stefan G, et al. "The Efficacy of Cognitive Behavioral Therapy: A Review of Meta-Analyses." *Cognitive Therapy and Research*, U.S. National Library of Medicine, 1 Oct. 2012, www.ncbi.nlm.nih.gov/pmc/articles/PMC3584580/.

12. Bouton, Mark E. "Why Behavior Change Is Difficult to Sustain." *Preventive Medicine*, U.S. National Library of Medicine, Nov. 2014, www.ncbi.nlm.nih.gov/pmc/articles/PMC4287360/.

13. Shand, Fiona L, et al. "What Might Interrupt Men's Suicide? Results from an Online Survey of Men." *BMJ Open*, U.S. National Library of Medicine, 15 Oct. 2015, www.ncbi.nlm.nih.gov/pmc/articles/PMC4611172/.

14. Gold, Joshua, and Joseph Ciorciari. "A Review on the Role of the Neuroscience of Flow States in the Modern World." *Behavioral Sciences (Basel, Switzerland)*, U.S. National Library of Medicine, 9 Sept. 2020, www.ncbi.nlm.nih.gov/pmc/articles/PMC7551835/.

15. Lin, Tzu-Wei, and Yu-Min Kuo. "Exercise Benefits Brain Function: The Monoamine Connection." *Brain Sciences*, U.S. National Library of Medicine, 11 Jan. 2013, www.ncbi.nlm.nih.gov/pmc/articles/PMC4061837/.

16. Vogel SW;Bijlenga D;Tanke M;Bron TI;van der Heijden KB;Swaab H;Beekman AT;Kooij JJ; "Circadian Rhythm Disruption as a Link between Attention-Deficit/Hyperactivity Disorder and Obesity?" *Journal of Psychosomatic Research*, U.S. National Library of Medicine, pubmed.ncbi.nlm.nih.gov/26526321/. Accessed 1 Dec. 2023.

17. Alhola, Paula, and Päivi Polo-Kantola. "Sleep Deprivation: Impact on Cognitive Performance." *Neuropsychiatric Disease and Treatment*, U.S. National Library of Medicine, 2007, www.ncbi.nlm.nih.gov/pmc/articles/PMC2656292/.

18. Gasmi, Amin, et al. "Neurotransmitters Regulation and Food Intake: The Role of Dietary Sources in Neurotransmission." *MDPI*, Multidisciplinary Digital Publishing Institute, 26 Dec. 2022, www.mdpi.com/1420-3049/28/1/210.

19. Derbyshire, E. "Do Omega-3/6 Fatty Acids Have a Therapeutic Role in Children and Young People with ADHD?" *Journal of Lipids*, U.S. National Library of Medicine, 2017, www.ncbi.nlm.nih.gov/pmc/articles/PMC5603098/.

20. Kim, Yujeong, and Hyeja Chang. "Correlation between Attention Deficit Hyperactivity Disorder and Sugar Consumption, Quality of Diet, and Dietary Behavior in School Children." *Nutrition Research and Practice*, U.S. National Library

of Medicine, June 2011, www.ncbi.nlm.nih.gov/pmc/articles/PMC3133757/.

21. Lakhan, Shaheen E, and Annette Kirchgessner. "Prescription Stimulants in Individuals with and without Attention Deficit Hyperactivity Disorder: Misuse, Cognitive Impact, and Adverse Effects." *Brain and Behavior*, U.S. National Library of Medicine, Sept. 2012, www.ncbi.nlm.nih.gov/pmc/articles/PMC3489818/.

22. Chang, Zheng, et al. "Stimulant ADHD Medication and Risk for Substance Abuse." *Journal of Child Psychology and Psychiatry, and Allied Disciplines*, U.S. National Library of Medicine, Aug. 2014, www.ncbi.nlm.nih.gov/pmc/articles/PMC4147667/.

23. Davis, Daphne M. "What Are the Benefits of Mindfulness?" *Monitor on Psychology*, American Psychological Association, www.apa.org/monitor/2012/07-08/ce-corner#:~:text=Researchers%20theorize%20that%20mindfulness%20meditation,to%20effective%20emotion%2Dregulation%20strategies. Accessed 12 Dec. 2023.

24. Gnanavel, Sundar, et al. "Attention Deficit Hyperactivity Disorder and Comorbidity: A Review of Literature." *World Journal of Clinical Cases*, U.S. National Library of Medicine, 6 Sept. 2019, www.ncbi.nlm.nih.gov/pmc/articles/PMC6745333/.

25. Komori, Teruhisa. "The Relaxation Effect of Prolonged Expiratory Breathing." *Mental Illness*, U.S. National Library of Medicine, 16 May 2018, www.ncbi.nlm.nih.gov/pmc/articles/PMC6037091/.